The Rosary
Prayer for All Seasons

Joanna Hastings, O.P.

Illustrations by Mary Rose Gimpl, O.P.
Foreword by Richard J. Sklba

A Liturgical Press Book

THE LITURGICAL PRESS
Collegeville, Minnesota

ACKNOWLEDGMENTS

Grateful acknowledgment is made to the following for permission to reproduce excerpts from these books:

Oxford University Press for Gerard Manley Hopkins, "The Windhover," and excerpts from "Ad Mariam," and "The May Magnificat," in *The Poems of Gerard Manley Hopkins*, edited by W. H. Gardner and N. H. McKenzie. © The Society of Jesus, 1967, 1970.

Oxford University Press for Verses 1-3 of "Now the Green Blade Riseth" from The Oxford Book of Carols, © 1964 Oxford University Press. Reprinted by permission of Oxford University Press.

The Methodist Publishing House, Abingdon Press, for one verse of Hymn 210, "If Thou But Suffer God to Guide Thee." Reprinted from *The Book of Hymns*, © 1964, 1966.

Christian Classics, Inc., and Sheed & Ward for two excerpts from "rhythms" of Caryll Houselander quoted in Maisie Ward, *Caryll Houselander: That Divine Eccentric*.

The Carmelite Sisters of Pewaukee, Wisconsin, for Jessica Powers, "The Pool of God," in *Selected Poetry of Jessica Powers*, edited by Regina Siegfried and Robert Morneau.

Unless otherwise noted, the biblical texts in this book are from the New Revised Standard Version Bible, copyright 1989, Division of Christian Education of the National Council of the Churches of Christ in the United States of America.

Cover: Our Lady of Vladimir, 12th-century Russian icon.
Design by Ann Blattner.

Copyright © 1993 by The Order of St. Benedict, Inc., Collegeville, Minnesota. All rights reserved. No part of this book may be reproduced in any form or by any means, electronic or mechanical, including photocopying, recording, taping, or any retrieval system, without the written permission of The Liturgical Press, Collegeville, Minnesota 56321. Printed in the United States of America.

2   3   4   5   6   7   8   9

Library of Congress Cataloging-in-Publication Data

Hastings, Joanna, 1937-
    The rosary : a prayer for all seasons / Joanna Hastings ; foreword by Richard J. Sklba ; illustrations by Mary Rose Gimpl.
        p.   cm.
    ISBN 0-8146-2134-1
    1. Mysteries of the Rosary—Meditations. 2. Catholic Church—Prayer-books and devotions—English. I. Title.
BT303.H36   1993
242'.74—dc20   92-43851
                                                                           CIP

DEDICATION

*to my mother,
Barbara Tanner Hastings,
in memory of my father,
John Douglas Hastings,
and of their great-granddaughter,
Jessica Marie Keller*

Contents

Foreword vii

Preface xi

Opening Prayers 1

Prologue: The Rosary . . . A Marvelous Prayer 3

Prayers of the Rosary 10

1. Behold the Handmaid of the Lord 11
2. Yours Shall Be Everlasting Joy 22
3. To You Is Born a Savior 33
4. My Eyes Have Seen Your Salvation 44
5. I Must Be in My Father's House 55

Interlude: Yours Is the Kingdom of God 66

6. My Soul Is Sorrowful Unto Death 77
7. He Was Despised and Rejected 88
8. Behold Your King 100
9. Take Up Your Cross and Follow Me 112
10. Why Have You Forsaken Me? 124

Interlude: Abide in My Love 135

11. On the Third Day He Will Rise Again 145
12. Declare His Glory Among the Nations 157

13.	My Peace I Give to You	170
14.	We Are God's Handiwork	182
15.	Christ in You, the Hope of Glory	193

Epilogue: Mother and Child 205

Concluding Prayers 212

Guide to Flower Illustrations 213

Foreword

Through the waters of baptism, the Spirit of God is indeed poured into our hearts, transforming us into the children of God (Romans 5:5 and 8:15f). By this saving grace the Church becomes the body of Christ and each of us his members. As a community and as individuals the events of our lives become infused with Christ's redemptive presence and associated with the mystery of his dying and rising in a profound manner. Consequently, everything human bears the imprint of eternity at its core and reflects the pattern of salvation in its unfolding. Everything human shines with the joy of the incarnation and reveals the brilliance of the glory to which the world is called in Christ.

The great grace of the rosary consists in its ability to open people's hearts to the major mysteries of Christ's life and thus to reveal the wonder present in our own lives each day. Pondering the Annunciation, for example, enables us to associate our every "yes" with Mary's acceptance of the Divine Will. Entering Elizabeth's house with Mary to become a silent witness to the greeting of these holy women discloses the presence of Christ in every family reunion or gesture of help to a relative in need.

Every disappointing rejection is associated with the sadness of Christ's passion; even the slightest mocking dismissal of our best efforts is clothed with a soldier's shabby scarlet cloak or crowned with the thistle-like acanthus leaves which mimic the golden laurel crown of kings. It is the Lord's passion which permeates our dying but also his glory which gives triumph to all our wounds and crowns them with Christ's final splendor.

Sister Joanna's prayer over the great mysteries of Christ in the rosary brings the richness of Dominican contemplation to this traditional treasure of popular spirituality. With a touch of poetry she weaves her own garland of images to accompany those who walk in this garden. There is nothing narrow in her glance as she ponders each mystery, for she reaches afar to complement the bouquet with biblical allusions and text. The work is a unique tribute to the grace of contemplative prayer in the Church. Like a perfume display in a department store or an herbal garden under the warm summer sun, this work represents an invitation to sample its fragrance.

The excerpts from Gerard Manley Hopkins, S.J., Caryll Houselander, Jessica Powers, or Annie Dillard provide a garnish for those who may treasure the verbal artistry and insight of these literary giants.

The very fact that Sister Joanna has included an interlude on the teachings of Jesus under the text "Yours Is the Kingdom of God" (Luke 6:20) between the Joyful and Sorrowful Mysteries, and also inserted another reflection on "Abide in My Love" (John 15:9) between the Sorrowful and Glorious Mysteries merits special comment here. In my judgment it represents an invitation to glean still other mysteries from the Gospels as we bring our lives into deeper union with Christ. A great and powerful journey into the mystery of Jesus can be explored by pondering the events which one could gather into new series, such as the teaching, healing, or praying mysteries, as well as the laughing, forgiving, or feeding mysteries of Christ. Even a series on the confronting mysteries of Christ's anger over arrogance or injustice might be explored. In any case, such new series enable every contemporary profession or occupation to find resonance with the traditional mysteries which the Gospels celebrated in the life of Christ.

The grace of prayer which introduces us into the major events of Christ is the opportunity truly to "imitate what these mysteries contain," as the prayer states, and "obtain what they promise."

May this journey with Mary, Mother of the Church and model of all disciples, enable the mystery of Christ to flourish in our world and bring forth the fruit of God's justice and peace everywhere.

Richard J. Sklba

Preface

"The Rosary," said Romano Guardini, "has the character of a sojourn." Praying the rosary calls one to move from the hustle and confusion of daily life into a more tranquil world where one may linger in the company of the Lord Jesus and his Mother, and be refreshed. The essays in this book attempt to provide support from Scripture and other sources for a sojourn with the mysteries of the rosary, the mysteries of our redemption in Christ.

Monsignor Guardini also commented, "The Rosary is not a road, but a place, and it has no goal but a depth." One prays the rosary in order to draw closer to God, to enter into deeper communion with him. Each of the essays on the fifteen rosary mysteries is based on its story in the Gospels. I have expanded, or deepened, the "place" of the story by incorporating other passages from the Bible, especially readings from the pertinent liturgical season or day of celebration.

Prayer makes a difference in Christian life. Communion with God transforms us, opens us to perceive deeper meaning in the words of Scripture. The stories of Jesus' life seen through the eyes of his Mother can guide the ways we live our commitment as Christians today. The essays thus include some reflection on the mysteries in Christian life. A prologue, two interludes, and a brief epilogue provide some continuity.

While prayer is the common ground of reader and author, each person's prayer is distinct. These essays thus reflect personal prayer, study, and experience. Each of them finds its own place. Their common ground is Scripture, liturgical season, and in most instances the climatic season of the northern year.

For the adult convert it is a tremendous, almost overwhelming experience to realize that one has received not only the gift of faith and fellowship in the Holy Spirit, but also new access to the magnificent treasures of wisdom and learning accumulated by the Church through the centuries. I have drawn on this heritage and deliberately have quoted material from Pope Paul VI and Pope John Paul II, from Documents of the Second Vatican Council, from theologians, exegetes, and spiritual writers, primarily of the twentieth century.

My understanding of Scripture and doctrine has been enlightened as well by the spoken word. The homilies of the Pallottine Fathers who serve as our chaplains often supplied welcome insights when they were needed. Retreat conferences preached to our community by Dominican fathers and brothers over the years offered new ideas or ways toward more profound reflection.

Michael Glazier suggested that someone in our community write a book on praying the rosary mysteries. I am grateful to him for the opportunity and for his confident patience during the process of planning and writing the book. The enthusiastic support of my family and of friends was most welcome. My thanks to them, and to Father Matthew Gottschalk, O.F.M.Cap., and to Father John Gerlach, O.P., for their interest and prayers.

To Mother Miriam Leonard, O.P., and to Sister Mary Thomas Ryan, O.P., I owe deep gratitude for their wisdom, knowledge, and patience in reading and preparing critiques of the essays at various stages of their development. My thanks also to Sister Mary Rose Gimpl, O.P., who drew the garden of graceful flowers to illustrate each of the mysteries, and to Sister Mary Timothy Dominique, O.P., and Sister Mary John Krupo, O.P., for their gracious help and their superb typing and proofreading skills. To all the sisters of my community, the Dominican Sisters of the Perpetual Rosary, my gratitude for their prayerful support, their patient interest, and their continuing demonstration of the love that flows from a life given to the Lord.

Joanna Hastings, O.P.
Milwaukee, Wisconsin
October 7, 1992

Opening Prayers

✝ God, come to my assistance.
Lord, make haste to help me.

Glory to the Father, and to the Son, and to the Holy Spirit:
as it was in the beginning, is now, and will be for ever.
Amen.

Hail, holy Queen, mother of mercy,
our life, our sweetness, and our hope.
To you do we cry,
poor banished children of Eve.
To you we send up our sighs,
mourning and weeping in this valley of tears.
Turn then, most gracious advocate,
your eyes of mercy toward us,
and after this exile
show us the blessed fruit of your womb, Jesus.
O clement, O loving,
O sweet Virgin Mary.

O Blessed Mother Mary, deign to accept our praises,
and protect us from your enemies.

Let us pray.

O God, whose only begotten Son, our Lord Jesus Christ, by his life, death, and resurrection has purchased for us the rewards of eternal life; grant, we beseech you, that in meditating in these mysteries of the most holy rosary of the Blessed Virgin Mary, we may come to imitate what they contain, and obtain what they promise; through the same Christ our Lord. Amen.

Prologue

The Rosary . . . A Marvelous Prayer
John Paul II

> We declare to you what was from the beginning, what we have heard, what we have seen with our eyes, what we have looked at and touched with our hands, concerning the word of life—this life was revealed, and we have seen it and testify to it, and declare to you the eternal life that was with the Father and was revealed to us—we declare to you what we have seen and heard so that you also may have fellowship with us; and truly our fellowship is with the Father and with his Son Jesus Christ.
>
> 1 John 1:1-3

The living Word of the living God is the heart of that marvelous prayer known to generations of Christians as the Rosary of Our Lady. An enduring prayer of great beauty, "marvelous in its simplicity and depth," the rosary opens a doorway to the world of Mary, the Mother of the Incarnate Word. What matters in the rosary is what mattered most to Mary: her son, Jesus. When we pray its mysteries, we see the events of his life through her eyes, and linger in the company of the mother who "kept all these things, pondering them in her heart" (Luke 2:19).

"The Holy Rosary," said John Paul II, "introduces us into the very heart of faith."[1] Its sequence and order reflect, as Paul VI commented, "the very way in which the Word of God, mercifully entering into human affairs, brought about the Redemption." Its joyful, sorrowful, and glorious mysteries set forth "the mystery of Christ in the very way in which it is seen by Saint Paul in the celebrated 'hymn' of the Letter to the Philippians—kenosis, death and exaltation (2:6-11)."[2]

The prayers of the rosary are drawn from Scripture. The words "become an arch in the sacred room of revelation, in which the truth of the living God is made known to us."[3] We enter the holy setting of each mystery repeating the prayer Jesus taught his disciples: "When you pray, say, 'Our Father who art in heaven. . . .'"

Within the sacred room, the decade of the mystery, we repeat the "Hail, Mary." The words draw one directly into the mystery of the incarnation. The first phrase echoes Gabriel's greeting to the Virgin of Nazareth. The next repeats the praise Elizabeth, filled with the Holy Spirit, cried when she heard Mary's greeting. In the concluding words we plead that the Mother of God will be with each of us in the essential moments of life, now and the hour of our death.

Each decade closes with praise of the Triune God who has revealed his love for us in this mystery of Jesus' life: Glory be to the Father, and to the Son, and to the Holy Spirit; as it was in the beginning, is now, and will be for ever. Amen.

The rosary incorporates the succession of these holy words and the telling of beads with moments of silence to form a background against which the fifteen mysteries of salvation unfold within the mind and heart. Far from being mere repetition of phrases, counting of prayers, or multiplication of words, the rosary is the Christian expression of an almost universal contemplative prayer tradition.

People of widely varying religious heritage have used beads or counters to guide and sustain their prayer for centuries. Madeleine L'Engle wrote, "To use beads with a prayer, Indian or Moslem or Christian, is to enflesh the words, make thought tangible. Unless misused, it is not in the realm of superstition but is an affirmation of creation, of all matter, of *ousia* [being]."[4] Father William Johnston calls the rosary "finger prayer," a prayer that engages the body as well as the mind and heart. Praying the rosary involves the whole person.

In every religion concerned with mystery one finds words and phrases repeated over and over in prayer. As they echo over and over in the mind, these words descend gradually to deeper levels of consciousness. In Christian spirituality the sacred word of centering prayer, the Jesus prayer, the chaste simplicity of Gregorian chant, short phrases from Scripture or liturgy, are all intended to draw the one praying into a more profound awareness of God's presence.

At these deeper levels the repetition of holy words becomes rhythmic, like waves upon a shore or the beat of one's heart. In time, the prayer becomes natural, a part of one's life, as essential as breathing out and breathing in. Rhythmic repetition is "the basic cadence that allows us to walk with Jesus and Mary without watching our feet." It liberates us, sets us "free to wander, to explore, to contemplate the mysteries that are the heartbeat of our lives."[5]

Indeed, the mysteries of the rosary embrace life itself. They are the rhythms of salvation, the songs of God's communion with his people. They lead one to spiritual awareness, mindfulness, and enlightenment, to knowledge, understanding, and wisdom, to union with God. Praying the rosary means entering into contemplative prayer centered in the mystery of the incarnation. We meet the God who reveals himself as love in the life, passion, death, resurrection, and exaltation of his Son, and who longs to draw us into communion with him.

Basically the rosary is a gospel prayer. But, while its content comes from the good news of Mark and Matthew, Luke and John, its fifteen mysteries form a continuum with the whole of salvation history. All of Scripture, the entire record of God's dealings with his people, contributes to one's understanding of Christ's life among us, and thus may lead one to explore new spiritual paths in praying the rosary.

The Book of Acts, which describes the struggles and triumphs of the apostolic Church, weaves a richly colorful, vivid tapestry of Christian life among the earliest believers. The experience of these sisters and brothers from a distant time and place provides a wonderful source for reflection and contemplation as we strive to live as Christians in our own day.

The letters written by Paul, Peter, James, and other first-century believers to guide the Churches they established contain some of the earliest treasures of our spiritual heritage. The wisdom and experience of these apostles and leaders still inform the life of the Church and guide twentieth-century disciples in understanding the words and deeds of our Lord.

The Hebrew Scriptures record the earliest treasures of salvation history: God's relationship with his people Israel, the Law, the Prophets, and the Writings or Wisdom. Both Old and New Testaments, inspired by the Spirit, enhance our realization of life transformed in Christ Jesus our Savior.

The rich biblical content of the rosary together with its focus on the world of Jesus and Mary make it a superb teaching prayer. The orderly sequence of the mysteries helps one remember the events of Christ's life interwoven with the responsive love and trust of his Mother who is the model for all Christians. Praying the rosary within the family, a prayer group, or a parish can become a rich learning experience for the individual believer and for the community. We enter the continuing prayer of the Church when we pray together the "common office of the people," as someone described the rosary.

The universal nature of the rosary appealed particularly to St. Dominic, Founder of the Order of Preachers. The simplicity of the prayer, the gospel content of the mysteries, the possibilities for silent meditation and deep reflection, the teaching and preaching potential, convinced Dominic that this was a prayer not only for him and for his nuns and friars, but also one beautifully suited to the people, the little ones to whom his Order would proclaim the gospel. Dominicans have prayed, taught, and preached the rosary, encouraging its spread among believers, ever since their founding in the thirteenth century.

As a prayer grounded in the Word of God, the rosary fosters spiritual growth by drawing us into the life of our Lord. Its holy words alternating with silent reflection inform Christian life by enriching communion with God. To little ones of every age, whom Jesus loved and to whom it is given to know the mysteries of the kingdom, the sacred words of the rosary become seeds sown in the rich, fertile soil of loving hearts. Just as the farmer casting seed into the earth looks forward to the harvest, so God's word "shall not return to me empty, but it shall accomplish that which I purpose, and succeed in the thing for which I sent it" (Isa 55:11).

Anyone whose life is transformed by an encounter with the living Word of the living God becomes fertile soil in which the seed of the Word takes root and begins to grow fruit for the final harvest. Prayer, communion with the Word, shelters, protects, and waters the growth of life in God. The rosary mysteries nourish faith, love, and hope in the deepest truths of our Christian heritage.

The person who prays discovers he or she cannot remain a mere student or spectator of Christian life. God's Word, alive and active, calls us to become part of the mystery, disciples of Christ, children of his Father, in brief, to become Christians, members of the believing community in whom God's Spirit dwells. God too looks toward the harvest and expects his people to bear the fruit of his gifts in the fullness of life.

Each of us grows and shares the fruits of our communion with God by the way we live. As one's experience of God deepens, his presence within becomes more apparent and more compelling. The memory of Jesus' life and of all that God has done for his people enriches our lives and overflows to enrich the lives of others. Prayerful meditation on the rosary mysteries sustains the communication of ourselves to others as graced, Spirit-filled friends of our Lord. Prayer marks the Church as a people united in communion with God and with one another.

In a very real sense, those who pray the rosary hold the world and all it contains within the loving, life-giving presence of Christ. They walk with the compassionate Lord who went among his people doing good. In his company the disciple becomes alert and hears the cry of the poor. The presence of the Lord urges one to heed the cry, to go out to help those in need. One who prays the rosary casts a lifeline of hope around the sick, suffering, anxious people of this harsh and struggling world.

Pondering the rosary mysteries with Mary, one also brings all that lies within one's own heart before God. As Jesus was the center of Mary's life, so also his concerns, his struggles and celebrations, his joys and griefs were hers. The people Jesus cared for were important to his Mother. The possibilities and ramifications here are endless, for Christ's love embraces the universe. No one stands beyond the outstretched arms of the crucified Lord; no one exists outside his Mother's love for the daughters and sons he gave to her care.

In the rosary we undertake a universal apostolate of prayer. Within that sacred arch of holy words we bring everything that concerns our life in this world. We praise and adore God the Father, Son, and Holy Spirit. We offer reparation for our sins and the sins of the world. We pray for the needs of others, for the cares and troubles of our time. We return thanks for all he has done for us.

The rosary celebrates God's abundant blessings and gifts, calling everyone to recognize the loving kindness of our God who sent his Son to share our earthly existence that we might share eternal life with him. It celebrates our faith and our heritage as Christ's people and urges us, "Rejoice in the Lord always" (Phil 4:4).

Mary's response to the good news of the Incarnate Word and to the demands Jesus' coming would make of her was an unequivocal *yes*. Praying the rosary helps us to respond as she did: to follow the way and truth and life of Christ; to enter into the loving communion of Father, Son, and Holy Spirit; and to receive the gift of salvation. In the rhythm and song of the rosary, in joy, sorrow, and the hope of glory, we hear the Word of God as heartbeat and life breath. When, like Mary, we keep it, we too are blessed.

NOTES

1. John Paul II, Angelus Address, October 29, 1978.
2. Paul VI, *Devotion to the Blessed Virgin Mary*, 45.
3. Romano Guardini, *The Rosary of Our Lady*, trans. H. von Schnecking (New York: P. J. Kenedy & Sons, 1955) 26.
4. Madeleine L'Engle, *The Summer of the Great-Grandmother* (San Francisco: Harper & Row, Publishers, 1974) 221.
5. Thomas Knobloch, O.P., "The Rosary and the Rhythm of God," *The Rosary Light & Life* (Jan.-Feb., 1990) 1.

Prayers of the Rosary

Our Father in heaven,
   hallowed be your name.
   Your kingdom come.
   Your will be done,
      on earth as it is in heaven.
Give us this day our daily bread;
And forgive us our debts,
   as we also have forgiven our debtors.
And do not bring us to the time of trial,
   but rescue us from the evil one.

Hail Mary, full of grace.
The Lord is with you.
Blessed are you among women.
And blessed is the fruit of your womb, Jesus.
Holy Mary, Mother of God,
Pray for us sinners
Now and in the hour of our death.
Amen.

Glory to the Father, and to the Son, and to the Holy Spirit:
As it was in the beginning, is now, and will be for ever.
                    Amen.

Annunciation of the Lord

Behold the Handmaid of the Lord

Luke 1:38

In the beginning God spoke. His Word borne on his Spirit, on the Breath of his mouth, moved over the black, turbulent waters of the earth, and brought order from chaos, light from darkness, the universe of being from nothingness. Word and Spirit are creative, bringing forth life where no life existed before. All that came to be was alive in the life-giving Word of God, alive on the wind-breath of the Spirit.

By the Breath of his mouth God gave life to the creatures he fashioned in his own image and likeness from the dust of the earth. He brought into being the man and the woman, companions, partners, children, bound to him by his Word and Spirit but always free to choose their own way.

In time the man and the woman broke their relationship with the Creator who gave them life. The familiar companionship no longer existed, for the Lord no longer walked with them in the garden of his creation during the cool of the day. And human beings, cast out from his presence, set their feet on the path that leads to death.

But the seed and the promise of life remained in them. The God who barred the way to the tree of life in Eden still cared for the beings formed by his hand and breathing his life, even as they walked away from him into the dark shadow of their disobedience and failure. From the wreckage God offered hope to fallen humanity. And in the fullness of time he sent his Word of life, his own Son, in the power of his Spirit to dwell in the midst of his people.

The Word is Christ, the image of the invisible God and the first born of all creation, completely divine and completely human. In the Incarnate Son, the Word made flesh, God bridges the abyss separating us from him and invites us to recover our relationship with him. He entered our human history by becoming one of us, and took our destiny upon himself.

> For God so loved the world that he gave his only Son,
> so that everyone who believes in him may not perish
> but may have eternal life.
> John 3:16

We celebrate the Annunciation of the Lord, the revelation of God's infinite love in the mystery of the incarnation, as the world spins from a time of darkness and death toward a season of hope and rebirth. In this time the winds of March blow harsh and chill across an empty landscape still held in the grey breath of winter. Frosty darts of sleet and rain sting the earth's surface, piling it with dense, hard layers of cold. Pale, drab, and silent, the empty land sways along a path swept by the wind.

Then suddenly the breath of winter dies. Sunlight breaks through the hardened surfaces and colors the landscape in a glow of warmth. Clouds and cold retreat; rivulets of melting snow converge in streams to water the frozen ground. Now the winds of March breathe life. The world awakes to springtime freshness, and the barren land is transformed. New life appears on the earth, growing and increasing under the warm light of the sun.

In this season between dying and rebirth, barrenness and fecundity, the angel Gabriel was sent from God to a city of Galilee in ancient Palestine. The city was Nazareth, an insignificant town in an obscure corner of the empire forged by Roman military might under the Caesars over two thousand years ago. Gabriel bore a message from God to a virgin of Nazareth. Her name was Mary, and she was betrothed to a man named Joseph, a descendant of the great King David. Following the custom of her time, Mary was living in the home of her family. When the year of betrothal ended, her marriage to Joseph would take place, and she would go to live with him.

According to traditional accounts, Mary was young at the time of the angel's appearance, perhaps no more than fifteen years old. Her tender, eager youthfulness, her growing relationship with Joseph, the excitement of her approaching marriage and the new responsibilities that would be hers, all contributed to the girl's feeling of joyful well-being. She was a daughter of Abraham, blessed by God. Life with all its wonderful possibilities spread out before her like the open fields of spring.

Then, as suddenly as the turn of a March wind, the angel Gabriel appeared and greeted her, "Greetings, favored one! The Lord is with you" (Luke 1:28). The angel's words greatly troubled Mary; she struggled to understand what sort of greeting this might be.

The angel reassured her, saying:

> Do not be afraid, Mary, for you have found favor with God. And now, you will conceive in your womb and bear a son, and you will name him Jesus. He will be great, and will be called the Son of the Most High, and the Lord God will give to him the throne of his

ancestor David. He will reign over the house of Jacob for ever, and of his kingdom there will be no end.

v. 30-33

Young as she was, Mary knew the history of her people and their longing for salvation. She grasped the meaning of the angel's message. The ancient promise, the word of hope, would be fulfilled through her. God had chosen her to be the mother of Israel's long-awaited Messiah. To the young virgin it seemed impossible that this wonderful deed would be accomplished through her. Seeking only to learn how she could do what God asked of her, Mary said to the angel, "How can this be, since I am a virgin?" (v. 34). The angel replied:

> The Holy Spirit will come upon you, and the power of the Most High will overshadow you; therefore the child to be born will be holy; he will be called the Son of God.
>
> v. 35

"And now," the angel continued, "your relative Elizabeth in her old age has also conceived a son; and this is the sixth month with her who was said to be barren. For nothing will be impossible with God" (vv. 36–37).

The pregnancy of the aging, childless wife of the priest Zechariah was a sign for Mary. Her own heritage had taught her to trust in the power and the promise of God who would bring forth life under circumstances impossible to overcome by merely human power. Caught up in the mystery that towered far above her, filled with the grace of God, Mary submitted her whole being to his will:

> Here am I, the servant of the Lord; let it be to me according to your word.
>
> v. 38

Simply and lovingly the young virgin of Nazareth received the Word of God. The Holy Spirit came upon her;

the power of the Most High overshadowed her; the Word became flesh within her and dwelt as Jesus of Nazareth among his people.

The story of the Annunciation reveals the grace of God appearing for the salvation of humankind. Everything about this mystery is grace. Salvation is the gracious gift of the God whose love transforms the fallen world and reconciles to himself the creatures so long estranged from him.

On the merely human level it is beyond hope that a virgin could conceive and bear a child. It would be impossible for Mary to be fruitful. As a virgin she resembles the barren fields of late winter, awaiting the warm winds of spring to breathe life from the wasteland. Only the overshadowing power of God, the Holy Spirit, the Breath on which the Word is borne, can bring forth life where no life can exist.

In ancient Israel barrenness or infertility was regarded as a curse, a failure to fulfill God's command to be fruitful and fill the earth. The childless wife was an object of scorn and reproach not only from her relatives but even from servants and slaves. On the human level her situation was hopeless; there was little she could do to alter the miserable circumstances of her barrenness.

But the God who formed the universe from nothingness can bring forth life from barren ground. The Hebrew Scriptures record stories of barren wives who, by the gracious power of God, gave birth to a child destined to contribute to the salvation of his people. The matriarchs of Israel, Sarah, Rebekah, and Rachel, are among the women whom God blessed with children; so too are Hannah, the mother of Samuel who was the last of Israel's judges, and the unnamed mother of the hero Samson.

Mary's kinswoman Elizabeth shared a distinction with the great matriarch Sarah, the childless wife of Abraham. Both women were well beyond their child-bearing years. Sarah was so old that she laughed when she heard the Lord tell Abraham, "I will surely return to you in due season, and your wife Sarah shall have a son." But the Lord demanded, "Is anything too wonderful for the Lord?" (Gen 18:10-15). And in fact, "Sarah conceived and bore Abraham a son in his old age, at the time of which God had spoken to him" (21:2). Abraham named the boy Isaac, *he will laugh* in Hebrew; for Sarah said, "God has brought laughter for me; everyone who hears will laugh with me" (v. 6).

To Elizabeth the conception of her child meant that the Lord had shown her great mercy. No longer would she be an object of scorn among family and neighbors; she and the child would be the center of rejoicing.

> Sing, O barren one who did not bear;
>   burst into song and shout,
>   you who have not been in labor!
> For the children of the desolate
>   woman will be more
> than the children of her that is
>   married, says the Lord.
>
> Isaiah 54:1

The once-barren Elizabeth is the sign for her young relative of God's blessing and power, but the exultant prophecy of Isaiah is marvelously fulfilled in Mary, far beyond any of Israel's expectations. The Holy Spirit, the power of the Most High, overshadowing the young virgin of Nazareth brought forth life in one whose state precluded the conception of a child. God's Word borne on his Breath became flesh in the womb of the virgin. From Mary, the Second Person of the Trinity took to himself a human nature, for to God nothing is impossible or too wonderful.

Jesus, the child of Mary, is thus completely divine and completely human. He is God emptying himself to be born of a woman and involving himself in humankind in order to share our dark destiny and deliver us from it. Jesus is in himself a new creation. "In Jesus, God has placed, in the midst of a barren, despairing mankind, a new beginning which is not a product of human history but a gift from above."¹

The Savior who comes to humankind from the mystery of the Triune God as pure gift must be received, and that too is grace. Mary's virginity is also an emptiness, a poverty of barrenness. Hers "is not a formless emptiness, a void without meaning; it has a shape, a form given to it by the purpose for which it is intended." Rather it is "like the hollow in the reed, the narrow riftless emptiness which can have only one destiny: to receive the piper's breath and to utter the song that is in his heart."²

Mary's response, "Here am I, the servant of the Lord; let it be with me according to your word," flowed eagerly and easily from the depths of a heart completely open to God. Hers was an emptiness formed to receive God's Word, give him flesh, and bear him into the world.

In his Encyclical on the Mother of the Redeemer John Paul II points out that Gabriel greets Mary not by her name but by a new name, "full of grace." This, he writes, is a special blessing. "In the mystery of Christ she is present even 'before the creation of the world,' as the one whom the Father has chosen as Mother of his Son in the Incarnation. And, what is more, the Son has chosen her, entrusting her eternally to the Spirit of holiness."³

Full of grace, Mary responded graciously. She "possessed above all the 'obedience of faith,' abandoning herself to the meaning which was given to the words of the Annunciation by him from whom they proceeded: God himself."⁴ Mary, her emptiness filled with grace, heard the word of the Lord and kept it. Overshadowed by the Spirit, she received the Word, the gift of God's salvation, so deeply and completely that he became flesh within the hollow of her being. She received the Christ as easily and quietly as the earth receives the springtime. Like the little reed, "the narrowest emptiness in the world," the Mother of our Savior, "utters infinite music."⁵

In the moment of her trusting surrender to the will of God, Mary became the focal point of salvation history. All that had gone before, the entire heritage of the people of God, the faith experience of her forebears stretching back to the great patriarch Abraham, prepared for this event and moved toward this young woman.

Mary belonged within the tradition of the faithful remnant, the true children of Abraham, who waited poor and powerless confidently hoping for the salvation of Israel. She is one of the faithful remnant of Israel, the *anawim* to whom God bends down with his life-giving love. Standing before God's messenger in the fresh flowering of young loveliness, Mary was the faithful Israel of the old covenant.

At the same time Mary embodied the new Israel. She is the holy daughter of Zion, the place where the hopes and longings of her people are fulfilled in the coming of Jesus Messiah.

> Sing aloud, O daughter Zion;
> shout, O Israel!
> Rejoice and exult with all your heart,
> O daughter Jerusalem!
> The King of Israel, the Lord, is
> in your midst.
>
> Zephaniah 3:14,15

The incarnation opened horizons far beyond the hopes of Israel and the promise of the old covenant. Mary was the first to follow her King and Lord beyond Israel's past dreams into the dawning reality of an eternal kingdom, a new and eternal covenant. When the Word became flesh in her womb, a new age began, the time of Emmanuel, of God-with-us. Mary became the place God had chosen for his dwelling in the midst of his people.

> This is my resting place forever;
> here I will reside, for I have desired it.
>
> Psalm 132:14

And in that moment of incarnation Mary stands for us. She is the Church, humankind responding in grace to the salvation God offers to everyone.

The young Mary became, as it were, the first Christian; her generous acceptance of her incomparable role in salvation history stands as *the* act of perfect discipleship. The Word of God came to her powerfully, overwhelmingly, and Mary opened her being in faith to receive him according to his will. She accepted what God asked of her without pausing to consult her own comfort or concern herself with the consequences of her assent to be the mother of his Son. Mary was entirely confident in the Lord and content simply to be his handmaid.

The response of Mary and everyone who receives the grace of salvation rises from the mysterious hidden center of the human person. It grows from the heart of an emptiness that can be filled by the Word borne on the Breath of the Spirit and formed into a new human being, a new creation. Where Christ finds a dwelling place of grace within us, there he can continue to transform the world and extend his kingdom to all peoples.

We do not know, as Mary surely did not know, what the Word borne on the Breath of the Spirit summons us to do or to become. As Jesus told the bewildered rabbi, Nicodemus, "The wind blows where it chooses, and you hear the sound of it, but you do not know where it comes from or where it goes. So it is with everyone who is born of the Spirit" (John 3:8). We simply trust that like Mary we will be open to the grace God offers us for the salvation of the world and respond to the overshadowing power of the Spirit with a measure of her simple trust and quiet greatness.

Ultimately one's response to God is a matter of faith. His grace works in us mysteriously, like the winds of March bringing forth new life from the winter wasteland of the earth. We may find it difficult to believe that the barren land frozen around the dead seeds of a past season will produce the harvest in the coming summer. But it is precisely from the poverty and emptiness of their decay and death that the land, warmed by the returning sun, will produce the fruits of new life.

God casts the seeds of grace, as the sower casts seeds of wheat. Some fall on rocky ground or a beaten path and fail to put down roots; some are choked by thorns and bramble. But the seed that falls into the rich soil of the loving heart sprouts and grows, hidden and mysterious. Few are aware of its presence until new life, new beauty, bursts from the darkness, much as the tender yellow blossoms break from the bare branches of a forsythia shrub in the first loveliness of spring.

Faith is a matter of work too. The hidden life must be nurtured and cherished; grace is offered again and again to be received; the way of salvation is never easy, and it must be chosen over and over in the course of a life.

By her *yes* to God Mary accepted responsibility for a tremendous work that demanded more of her than ordinary motherhood. She would give God's Son a human nature, the flesh in which he would become like us in all things but sin. He would see the earth with the eyes she gave him, walk its hills, its fields, its highways with human feet. His skilled, sensitive carpenter's hands, hands that later brought healing to the sick and suffering, came from her. The ears that heard the cries of the poor, the sick, and the dying with such compassion were human ears. In flesh like hers he endured his agony and passion; in that flesh he was raised by the Spirit's power to the eternal glory of God.

All this was still to come. In the moment of the incarnation Mary stood alone in the fresh blossoming of springtime loveliness before the God of Abraham, Isaac, and Jacob. In her the longing of all humankind was fulfilled: the Word became flesh; through her he dwelt among us that we might see his glory not only in Mary but in each other.

Our Lady, the highly favored one, the beloved daughter Zion, is always one of us. She is our example, our model, the woman of faith. She is, in a sense, the gift of ourselves to God, for she did what we also try to do: receive God's Word borne on his Spirit, and bear his Son into the world. With her let us proclaim with loving, unwavering confidence, "Here am I, the servant of the Lord; let it be with me according to your word."

NOTES

1. Joseph Cardinal Ratzinger, *Introduction to Christianity*, trans. J. R. Foster (New York: The Seabury Press, 1968) 211.
2. Caryll Houselander, *The Reed of God* (New York: Sheed & Ward, 1944) 3.
3. *Mother of the Redeemer*, 8.
4. Ibid., 15.
5. Houselander, *The Reed of God*, 11.

Visitation

Yours Shall Be Everlasting Joy
(Isaiah 61:7)

The Church celebrates the feast of the Visitation at the end of May, Mary's month. The winter has passed. What seemed impossible in its barren landscape now is reality in the radiant light of spring. The earth has come to life again.

> And May has come, hair-bound in flowers,
> With eyes that smile thro' the tears of the hours,
> With joy for today and hope for to-morrow
>   And the promise of Summer within her breast![1]

Happiness blossoms with the May-time flowers in a wild exuberance of beauty. Their loveliness spreads through parks and playgrounds, in gardens and fields, across the hillsides, and along woodland trails. Warmed in the fire of the returning sun, the air surrounds us with the gentle fragrance of things in bloom. The land, washed in the snow and rain of colder months, shines in the beauty of creation renewed and bursting forth after a season of rest and death. And living things, newly born, hatched, or sprung from the earth, grow at an astonishing rate. Birds return to sing, and children, released like coiled springs from the restraining grip of winter, race and shout and laugh as they play.

The coming of May calls everyone to welcome the new hope flowering from the earth, to be part of the moments that fill the heart with so much joy that there is no room for anything else. The vibrant activity of the earth in spring spreads a glow of freshness and joy over everything. It is a happiness to be remembered when new life grows to maturity, bears its fruit, and fades down under the relentless turning of the year into another season of winter.

As a lamp on a lampstand gives light to all in the house during the dark time of year, so the coming of spring brings light for all the world to see the wonder of God's creation. May surrounds us again with the love God has for everything that he made, the creation that he saw was very good.

> Arise, my love, my fair one,
> and come away;
> for now the winter is past,
> the rain is over and gone.
> The flowers appear on the earth;
> the time of singing has come,
> and the voice of the turtledove
> is heard in our land.
> The fig tree puts forth its figs,
> and the vines are in blossom;
> they give forth fragrance.
> Arise, my love, my fair one,
> and come away.
>
> Canticle 2:10-13

And thus in May we celebrate Our Lady who arose and went with haste from her home in Nazareth into the hill country, to a city of Judea, and to the home of her kinswoman Elizabeth. Coming fresh from her encounter with the messenger of God, Mary journeyed surrounded by the full loveliness of spring, aware that new life was beginning to form and grow within her.

> What is Spring?
> Growth in everything—
>
> Flesh and fleece, fur and feather,
> Grass and greenworld all together;
> > Star-eyed strawberry-breasted
> > Throstle above her nested
>
> Cluster of bugle blue shells thin
> Forms and warms the life within;
> > And bird and blossom swell
> > In sod or sheath or shell.
>
> All things rising, all things sizing
> Mary sees, sympathizing
> > With that world of good,
> > Nature's motherhood.
>
> Their magnifying of each its kind
> With delight calls to mind
> > How she did in her stored
> > Magnify the Lord.
>
> . . .
>
> This ecstasy all through mothering earth
> Tells Mary her mirth till Christ's birth
> > To remember and exultation
> > In God who was her salvation.[2]

The joyful wonder of the season touched Mary's kinswoman too, for Elizabeth also was the bearer of new life. An older woman, a barren wife and a sign of God's disfavor as far as her neighbors were concerned, Elizabeth had conceived a son. Unknown to anyone except Mary, she was in the sixth month of her pregnancy at the time of her young cousin's visit. When they met, each woman was gratefully aware that the life to which she would give birth was all God's doing. Elizabeth had said in her joy, "This is what the Lord has done for me when he looked favorably on me and took away the disgrace I have endured among my people" (Luke 1:25). What seemed impossible for the barren wife or the young virgin was not impossible for God.

Mary's visit to Elizabeth often is pondered simply on the basis of the help and comfort she so generously offered to her older kinswoman. But Elizabeth in her turn had much to offer Mary. At the time she was the only person with whom Mary could share her remarkable news and be assured of understanding. It is no wonder the younger woman made the long, difficult journey from Nazareth to the hill country of Judea in haste. As Gabriel told her, the older woman would be a sign to Mary that her own deep experience and her assent to the angel's call were real. Her eager faith was enough to send her hurrying to share with Elizabeth the wonder of all that God had done for her.

Then Mary arrived and entered the house. As she greeted Elizabeth, it became apparent that God's presence within her was so vibrant, so radiant, that explanations were superfluous. Elizabeth, caught up by the Spirit who filled the child in her own womb, already shared the amazing news. A joyful excitement rings in Elizabeth's song of praise:

> Blessed are you among women, and blessed is the fruit of your womb. And why has this happened to me, that the mother of my Lord comes to me? For as soon as I heard the sound of your greeting, the child in my womb leaped for joy. And blessed is she who believed that there would be a fulfillment of what was spoken to her by the Lord.
>
> Luke 1:42-45

In the exultant meeting of Mary and Elizabeth we experience the awesome reality of the incarnation. The two women were signs to each other that God was fulfilling his promise of salvation for all peoples. It is as though heaven and earth meet again in little space where the mysterious power of God's creative power became manifest in two daughters of Abraham. As Mary and Elizabeth greeted one another, they embodied all the joyful, confident hope of springtime. The bright, fresh radiance of their meeting shines down the centuries through the words of Luke's story. It is the exultant happiness of human beings caught up in the wonder of God's love for them.

For Mary and Elizabeth there was also the realization that the new life each held within her meant salvation and hope for the people of Israel. In that moment the joy of May burst forth in songs of springtime praise between these two women blessed by the Most High God.

Mary brought the Christ to her older kinswoman. His Spirit leaping in the unborn John radiated through his mother, filling Elizabeth with the presence of the Lord. Theirs was a vibrant witness to their faith in the abiding goodness of God and their confidence in his kindness and mercy. Elizabeth, still wrapped in the wonder of her own miracle, sang out her joy in praise of Mary, the one who believed that the Lord's word to her would be fulfilled. But Mary's exultant song glorified the Lord who had blessed her so wonderfully.

> My soul magnifies the Lord,
>   and my spirit rejoices in God
>   my Savior,
> for he has looked with favor on
>   the lowliness of his handmaiden.
>   Surely, from now on all
>   generations will call me blessed;
> for the Mighty One has done
>   great things for me,
>   and holy is his name.
>
> Luke 1:46-49

Filled with the grace of God, his handmaid turned the praises of Elizabeth away from herself toward the mighty and merciful One who had done such great things for her and through her for Israel. In the light of her own blessed state Mary sees the compassionate power of God reversing the life-situation of his people. He scatters the proud, pulls the mighty from their thrones, and lifts up the lowly and the humble. The hungry he fills with good things, but the rich and the well-fed who have no need of him he sends away empty. God had not forgotten Israel; in his mercy he remembered his people and all that he promised centuries before, to Abraham and his posterity forever.

Somehow it seemed that all Israel, all the peoples of earth, rejoiced in the Spirit-filled meeting of Mary and Elizabeth. Even as the young virgin responded for Israel and for us to God's call, so the older woman whom God blessed so greatly received the news for us. She believed for us in the Lord's Word which she experienced as the Spirit filled the child in her womb. Mary and Elizabeth, women of faith, sang out their joy in the Lord as Isaiah urged some centuries earlier:

> Sing praises to the Lord, for he has
>   done gloriously;
> let this be known in all the earth.
> Shout aloud and sing for joy,
>   O royal Zion,
> for great in your midst is the
>   Holy One of Israel.
>
> Isaiah 12:5-6

Surely the splendor of Mary's *Magnificat* reflects the joy and the gratitude she experienced when she met her kinswoman and recognized the sign given her by the angel. Joy arose too when she realized moments later that the Spirit who had overshadowed her was giving the wonderful, almost incredible good news to Elizabeth. And the unborn John received the fulfillment of the angel's promise to his father Zechariah, "Even before his birth he will be filled with the Holy Spirit" (Luke 1:15).

> Bless God and acknowledge him in the presence of all the living for the good things he has done for you. Bless and sing praise to his name.
>
> Tobit 12:6

The good news of Jesus Christ, the Son of God, begins here, proclaimed in joy by the two women and by their unborn sons. Elizabeth, even when she realized that God had given her the child she longed to have, perhaps still wondered if the miracle could be real. Mary in her turn set forth at once to share the presence of Christ within her. He was the world's salvation, the true light that enlightens everyone, a presence that cannot be hidden.

To Elizabeth and the unborn John, Mary's voice sang like the piercingly sweet music of shepherd's pipes or temple bells sounding gently on the warm breeze of a May evening. Her greeting heralded the presence of the Holy Spirit, calling and awakening the unborn John and making him a prophet from his mother's womb. His mission began in the moment he received the Spirit and proclaimed the coming of Christ, the Word of God, in his leap of joy. Jesus himself began his own ministry when his mother saw and greeted Elizabeth. As the source of the Holy Spirit, he radiated the good news of salvation.

Mary truly is *Theotokos*, God-bearer, and the first disciple of her son. She did nothing to convey her news to Elizabeth; she made no gesture, spoke no word of her good news, sent no advance message of her visit. She simply appeared at her kinswoman's house and greeted her. God himself, who cannot be contained, revealed his presence through his handmaid.

The mother of Jesus received the Word willingly and faithfully, as the earth receives the warm rains that mark the coming of spring. Her being was open to God's call. She became luminous in the light of God's grace. The work of salvation belonged to her son, but she became the means by which he accomplished it.

Mary's *yes* to God set her not only on the journey into Judea and the house of Zechariah and Elizabeth, it also determined the pilgrimage she would undertake during her life. She began it in wonder and continued it in the joy so filling her own finite being that it became a song of exultant praise in communion with another graced woman in the presence of the Holy Spirit of God.

The good news of salvation is given us in the myriad ways God makes his presence among us known. He is joy, love, and peace within our heart of hearts; he is with us in the beauty of creation, with us in the love we have for him and for one another. The noted Methodist preacher, Ernest Fremont Tittle, commented, "What the soul magnifies makes a vast difference in human life."[3] Because we are Christians, believers, we are graced persons to whom God has given the word of his kingdom and in whom he has planted the seed of his coming reign. Through his Spirit his Son dwells within us. Through us he comes to others, because in our lives we try to proclaim his greatness, because our souls magnify the Lord.

Indeed, the good news must be proclaimed and shared. Everyone who bears the Word of God within his or her being experiences that ardent, burning presence urging one forward, revealing itself as one lives the good news of his kingdom in the company of others. Indeed the marvelous joy of fellowship and communion is the common heritage of all peoples who believe that the words God has spoken to us will be fulfilled.

Then with Mary and Elizabeth we cry praise aloud to the surrounding hills. For the good news summons us to enter the kingdom of God, to become members of his family.

> To all who received him, who believed in his name,
> he gave power to become the children of God.
> John 1:12

This is a great mystery: we become children of God, his daughters and sons by adoption, brothers and sisters of our Lord Jesus. We are free to live in his peace and to grow in the warm light of his grace. We know and live the gospel not in isolation but with company of believers in every time and place.

In his public ministry Jesus preached the kingdom throughout the countryside of Galilee and Judea, but he also quickly gathered disciples, followers whom he trained and then sent out to preach the good news in their turn. The early apostolic community shared the joy of Christ's presence:

> All who believed were together and had all things in common. Day by day, as they spent much time together in the temple, they broke bread at home and ate their food with glad and generous hearts, praising God and having the goodwill of all the people.
>
> Acts 2:44, 46-47

The Apostle Paul exclaimed to his converts and friends in the Christian community at Philippi:

> I thank my God every time I remember you, constantly praying with joy in every one of my prayers for all of you, because of your sharing in the gospel from the first day until now.
>
> Philippians 1:3-5

He held these beloved brothers and sisters in his heart, for "all of you share in God's grace with me." Paul exclaimed, "For God is my witness, how I long for all of you with the compassion of Christ Jesus" (vv. 7, 8).

All of us share in this joyful affection, in the grace and love of our God who comes to make his home within us. Then the good news of God-with-us can spread like spring flowers covering the hillsides in beauty and light. And that is cause for great joy no one can take from us. "Rejoice in the Lord always," Paul urged his friends at Philippi, "and again I say, Rejoice!" Everyone must know how happy you are, for the Lord is near. (See Phil 4:4, 5.)

God's Word is the seed planted within the heart of every human person. When we allow the seed to grow, as the earth allows the fresh, bright growth of spring, Christ's life in us also grows. Our hearts open to become the dwelling place of God in the Spirit. Where the Spirit dwells, nothing is solitary, hidden, or sad. Everything shines forth in the joyful light of salvation. Christ Jesus becomes an urgent presence within us, reaching out, seeking to touch, sharing the good news of the kingdom, sharing the joy of our fellowship in the Spirit with everyone we meet.

The great privilege of our communion in Christ our Lord brings us the joy of becoming God-bearers for one another. We become ambassadors for Christ, going out to others from the center of that fellowship we have shared with him. Like Andrew, one of the first disciples, who followed Jesus to see where he stayed and then came to tell his brother, Simon Peter, he had found the Messiah; like Philip who found Nathaniel and took him to Jesus (John 1:38, 39, 41, 45, 46), we call each other by our faith in the Christ who dwells within.

Then, like Mary, we set out in haste to proclaim the good news, rejoicing in the presence of the Lord and the gifts of faith, love, and hope he has given to us in such abundance, and through us to all the world. As we have received him through his Spirit, so like Mary we can allow his joyful presence to grow within us.

> Let the Son of God grow in thee, for he is formed in thee. Let Him become to thee a great smile and exultation and perfect joy which no man can take from thee.[4]

NOTES

1. Gerard Manley Hopkins, "Ad Miriam," W. H. Gardner and N. H. MacKenzie, *The Poems of Gerard Manley Hopkins*, 4th edition (New York: Oxford University Press, 1970) 37.

2. Gerard Manley Hopkins, "The May Magnificat," *The Poems of Gerard Manley Hopkins*, 77. "Throstle" refers to the type of bird more commonly known as a thrush. The American robin is an example.

3. Ernest Fremont Tittle, *The Gospel According to Luke: Exposition and Application* (New York: Harper & Brothers Publishers, 1951) 7.

4. Isaac D'Etoile, quoted in Thomas Merton, *Silence in Heaven: A Book of the Monastic Life* (New York: The Studio Publications, Inc., in association with Thomas Y. Crowell Co., 1955) 30.

Birth of Jesus

To You Is Born a Savior
Luke 2:11

Silence bends the night in hollows
of expectation.
Fields disappear, and darkness
murmurs among the drowsy sheep.
The land is open, exposed, waiting
under the black and starry sky,

where shepherds watch over their flock,
listening, listening to the night, waiting
for dawn (as Israel waits for the Lord),
while a sleeping world whirls its course
through the vast eternal silence of space.

    The dying year slowly winds from autumn into winter, and darkness commands more of the day than does the light. The sun rises from the long cold nights over a barren landscape, symbolizing a world and a people caught and groaning in humanity's ancient choice of sin.
    Then, as the northern hemisphere tilts to its most distant point from the sun, the earth begins to spin its darkened, colder realms back toward the source of light and warmth.

God's gift, the word of light spoken over the chaos of the primeval earth, does not cease, for "God saw that the light was good" (Gen 1:4). Even when the rebellion of humankind wrapped a deeper darkness over creation God's light, like the sun, remained in his promise of salvation, and it was good.

Today, when technological marvels can push back the harsh realities of winter nights, we long for the return of the sun's light and warmth. From our darkness we yearn for the coming of salvation and the Messiah who brings life and hope.

> Out of the depths I cry to you, O Lord.
> > Lord, hear my voice!
> Let your ears be attentive
> > to the voice of my supplications!
>
> I wait for the Lord, my soul waits,
> > and in his word I hope;
> my soul waits for the Lord
> > more than those who watch for the morning.
> > > Psalm 130:1-2, 5-6

The Lord to whom we cry is the God of mercy, who hears the voice of his people. As surely as those who watch through the night will see the coming of dawn, and as the darkest night gives way to the brighter morning of the returning sun; so also the people who walk in darkness will see a great light, and on those who dwell in a land of darkness light will shine. (See Isa 9:2.)

The God who called light from darkness in time sent his Son to be light and life to humankind. The fulfillment of his promise breaks upon the earth quietly, simply, but with a radiance that almost takes one's breath away, even as the stars of heaven, a myriad of suns, break through the clouds of a winter night in overwhelming brilliant beauty.

Each year we welcome God's Son into our hearts and lives just after the winter solstice, when the night is pushed back by the sun's return. And when that night is darkest, at midnight, we celebrate the birth of Jesus our Savior, rejoicing over and over at his coming into our world and our history in the ancient city of Bethlehem.

> O little town of Bethlehem,
> How still we see thee lie!
> Above thy deep and dreamless sleep
> The silent stars go by;
> Yet in the dark streets shineth
> The everlasting light;
> The hopes and fears of all the years
> Are met in thee tonight.[1]

On the night of Jesus' birth, the night when, "The true light, which enlightens everyone was coming into the world" (John 1:9), so many people crowded into normally quiet Bethlehem that late arrivals found no room in the inn or caravanserai. They were forced instead to find meager comfort where they could, in rough animal shelters hollowed out of the city's surrounding hills.

The unusual influx of travelers was the direct result of an imperial decree. The Roman Emperor Augustus had ordered a census in which "all the world should be registered" (Luke 2:1). Every person living within the vast Empire was to return to his city of origin, together with his family and dependents, there to be registered in the tax rolls of Rome.

Into the confusion and turmoil of many people on the move came a young couple from Nazareth in Galilee. Obedient to Caesar's decree, Joseph and Mary had made the long journey to the city of David. By the time they arrived, Bethlehem was more than crowded. Eventually Joseph managed to find a makeshift shelter for Mary, "who was expecting a child" (v. 5).

> While they were there, the time came for her to deliver her child. And she gave birth to her firstborn son and wrapped him in bands of cloth, and laid him in

> a manger, because there was no place for them in the inn.
>
> Luke 2:6-7

The Son of the Most High, the heir to King David's throne, the Holy One of God was born in the shadowy obscurity of a hillside stable in David's city under the stars of a winter night. He came in the stillness to dwell among his people, welcomed and cherished by Mary and Joseph even in the rough poverty of his birthplace. The king, the "one who is to rule in Israel" (Mic 5:2), returned to Bethlehem, to the city from which the great David had gone forth from his anointing long before.

The mystery of Jesus' coming fills the world and its history. It radiates beyond our limited human sight into the infinite reaches of the universe. In the helpless, newborn baby sleeping in a manger our God entered human history. Eternity entered time, caught it up, and made it holy in God's own time that is eternal life. God indeed did something new. The Creator who made us in his image and likeness called every human being into new relationship with him.

As part of his creation we are intimately related to the Word who was with God in the beginning. In Jesus, the Word became flesh, the weak, fragile, mortal stuff of human existence. The Word descended to be the new, earth-bound presence of God among his people. In becoming Emmanuel, God-with-us, the Son subjected himself to all that binds human life in order to free us for salvation.

> Christ Jesus,
> > though he was in the form of God,
> > > did not regard equality with God
> > > as something to be exploited,
> >
> > but emptied himself,
> > > taking the form of a slave,
> > > being born in human likeness.
>
> Philippians 2:6-7

Even in the form of a fragile, mortal human infant Jesus is the Son of the Most High. "He is the reflection of God's glory and the exact imprint of God's very being, and he sustains all things by his powerful word" (Heb 1:3). The awesome mystery of the Word made flesh is manifested in the glory visible in the face of Christ. "And the Word became flesh and lived among us, and we have seen his glory, the glory as of a father's only son, full of grace and truth" (John 1:14).

For Luke that glory appeared in the heavens, as though the stars shining down on Bethlehem that night split the sky with their radiance, and angels descended in their light. The divine mystery glowed on a cosmic scale that the great glad tidings might be proclaimed and the rejoicing of the universe shared with everyone.

Jesus later would warn his disciples, "Blessed are those slaves whom the master finds alert when he comes" (Luke 12:37). On the night of his birth the alert ones were shepherds living in the fields outside Bethlehem, keeping watch over their flock by night.

> Then an angel of the Lord stood before them, and the glory of the Lord shone around them, and they were terrified. But the angel said to them, "Do not be afraid; for see—I am bringing you good news of great joy for all the people; to you is born this day in the city of David a Savior, who is the Messiah, the Lord.
> Luke 2:9-11

Then suddenly a multitude of the heavenly host appeared in the skies overhead. The great angelic choir sang praise to God: Glory to God in the highest and on earth peace to all peoples of good will. (See v. 14.)

The shepherds responded immediately. When the angels had gone away from them into heaven, they set out for Bethlehem to see for themselves "this thing that has taken place, which the Lord has made known to us" (v. 15). They found the baby lying in the manger just as the angel had foretold. When they had seen the child, they told Mary and Joseph of the angels and their message; then they returned to their flock, glorifying and praising God.

> For Christ is born of Mary,
> And gathered all above,
> While mortals sleep, the angels keep
> Their watch of wond'ring love.
> O morning stars, together
> Proclaim the holy birth,
> And praises sing to God the King,
> And peace to men on earth.

The watching shepherds saw the blaze of God's glory across the skies above their field on Christmas night. But in Matthew's Gospel that light appeared in a far-off land east of Palestine, in a single point. Before the birth of Jesus wise men in that distant region, who studied the heavens and pondered their mysteries, were alert and watching as a new star rose in the east. They realized its significance, and their response was as prompt as that of the shepherds; they set out to follow the star's course.

The long journey brought the wise men to Jerusalem and the court of Herod the Great. There they inquired, "Where is the child who has been born king of the Jews? For we observed his star at its rising, and have come to pay him homage" (Matt 2:2). Learning from Herod and his court that the child was to be born in Bethlehem, the wise men continued their journey.

> And there, ahead of them, went the star that they had seen at its rising, until it stopped over the place where the child was.
>
> Matthew 2:9

When the wise men saw that the star had stopped, "they were overwhelmed with joy." The unlikely surroundings of the child and his family failed to sway their conviction that here indeed was the king they had traveled so far to worship. The light of heaven shining through the star was their guide. In deep faith the wise men knelt down before the Lord, paid him homage, and offered him kingly gifts of gold, frankincense, and myrrh. Then, warned in a dream not to return to Herod's court, they quietly "left for their own country by another road" (vv. 10, 12).

The first people to hear the good news were awake, open in their own ways to respond with eagerness to see the wonderful child for themselves. They were ready to believe, to offer their homage, and to rejoice, praising God for all he had made known to them. The shepherds in their simplicity, the wise men in their knowledge, were alert to the mysteries God revealed to them in and through creation. They beheld the light of God's glory shining in the tiny face of a baby whose bed was a manger in a hillside cave.

For a world weighed down with material things and burdened by pompous pride, the sign of the manger means little beyond a certain touching poverty. It does not signify kingly dignity and honor. For those open to receive the light of God, the manger is a sign of kingly dignity and honor, a confirmation of God's gift to people of faith and good will.

Mary, Joseph, and the shepherds were subject to the whims of a Roman emperor and the tyranny of Roman military might. With the coming of the Savior their lives suddenly were thrust upon the stage of history. At the time, news of Jesus' birth made little ripple on the firm surface of the Roman occupation; the baby was just one more potential taxpayer. The wise men, on the other hand, left their quiet studies and traveled a great distance only to find themselves unwittingly plunged into the hotbed of political intrigue and court scandal that characterized the violent reign of Herod the Great.

The tetrarch and all Jerusalem were troubled by the request of the Eastern travelers for information. If the child was the king of the Jews, if he was the Messiah, he threatened Herod's power. In a furious rage after realizing the wise men had returned to their own land without telling him where they had found the child, Herod had every boy in Bethlehem under two years of age killed. Jesus escaped his wrath, because Joseph, warned by an angel of the Lord in a dream, fled with him and his mother to Egypt, where they remained in exile until Herod was dead.

The violent response of Herod and his court contrasts starkly and grimly with the praise and worship offered by the men and women who received the good news of Jesus' birth with such joy. The Prologue of John's Gospel notes sadly:

> The true light, which enlightens everyone, was coming into the world. He was in the world, and the world came into being through him; yet the world did not know him. He came to what was his own, and his own people did not accept him.
>
> John 1:10-11

His name is Jesus, *Yeshua*, he who saves his people. His coming in the likeness of humankind is God's offer of salvation. The Savior is the perfect gift of his Father to human beings. Jesus himself is the perfect response of humankind to that gift. His presence among us is the Word of God echoing through our complacency, calling us, waking us from our night. His coming demands that we make a choice: to receive him and so receive power to become children of our God, or to reject him and cling desperately to our darkness.

When we do receive the Christchild, we enter his world, and join the quiet, simple, yet valiant company of Mary and Joseph, of shepherds and wise men. It is a world peopled by faithful women and men who wait for the Lord, trusting that he will fulfill his promises however they have been given. Leaving their flock on the hillside, the shepherds went in haste to rejoice and marvel at a baby lying in a manger. The wise men traveled a long, hard way to worship a small child. Joseph, abandoning home and livelihood, risked the dangers of a hasty flight through the wilderness to Egypt in order to protect the child. Mary, obedient as always to God's will, treasured all these things and pondered them in her heart. God's Word, his offer of salvation, challenges us at the same time it cherishes us in his peace and love.

> How silently, how silently,
> The wondrous gift is given!
> So God imparts to human hearts
> The blessings of his heav'n.
> No ear may hear his coming,
> But in this world of sin,
> Where meek souls will receive him still
> The dear Christ enters in.

The Christchild truly is peace for those who are troubled, lost, or ill with the sin of the world around them. He is God's gift of love binding us to the One who loved us and sent his Son to tell us who and what he really is, to make us know him as he is for us.

Jesus reveals what it means to be in communion with God. He shows us the way to enter into new, life-giving relationship with our loving, merciful Father. The mystery of human life, wrapped in the truth and love of God, was opened and revealed on that holy night in his Son.

> The truth is that only in the mystery of the Incarnate Word does the mystery of man take on light. Christ, by the revelation of the Father and his love, fully reveals man to man himself and makes his supreme calling clear.[2]

In Christ we fallen creatures of God are lifted up and set right with our heavenly Father. In him we take up the journey of faith along the path that leads to fullness of life in his presence.

> For it is the God who said, "Let light shine out of darkness," who has shone in our hearts to give the light of the knowledge of the glory of God in the face of Jesus Christ.
>
> 2 Corinthians 4:6

Each year we keep the feast of Christmas, lighting candles against the darkness of winter and singing songs of joyful praise, "Today is born our Savior, Christ the Lord." In the light of Christ's coming we too are born *today* with the new creation. If we receive him, we can be filled with his light and grace. When we allow him to be visible in us, to live and work in us, and to offer his peace and love through us, he is born again in the world he came to save.

As Mary radiated Christ's presence to Elizabeth, as the tiny baby revealed the splendor of God's glory to shepherds and wise men, so our lives may become centers of his light, candles glowing through the dust and darkness of the world's turmoil. And we are needed. Annie Dillard put it bluntly:

> When the candle is burning, who looks at the wick? When the candle is out, who needs it? But the world without light is wasteland and chaos, and a life without sacrifice is abomination.[3]

Jesus later would exclaim to his disciples, "I have come to bring fire to the earth!" (Luke 12:49). He sets us like candles lit by the Word of God, each face, "flame like a seraph's, lighting the kingdom of God for people to see, ..."[4]

The heavens tell the glory of God. The stars of Christmas night proclaim the light that is Christ coming into the world. The stars are symbols as well, of countless witnesses to the salvation offered us in Jesus born of Mary. If we are, as he told us, "the light of the world" (Matt 5:14), the fire our Lord has kindled on earth will burn in our lives to warm and enlighten all whom we love, all for whom and with whom we live.[5] Through the cold, the dust, and the despair of a world struggling in hatred, churned by greed and violence, the Christchild shines like a great sweep of light flinging the glowing sparks of God's love into the hearts of all who welcome his coming.

> O holy Child of Bethlehem!
> Descend to us, we pray;
> Cast out our sin and enter in,
> Be born in us today.
> We hear the Christmas angels
> The great glad tidings tell;
> O come to us, abide with us,
> Our Lord Emmanuel!

NOTES

1. Phillips Brooks, 1867.
2. *Pastoral Constitution on the Church in the Modern World*, 22.
3. Annie Dillard, *Holy the Firm* (New York: Harper & Row, 1977) 72.
4. Ibid.
5. Daniel Morrissey, O.P., Homily, July 4, 1975.

Presentation of the Lord

My Eyes Have Seen Your Salvation
Luke 2:30

Great events quickly become history; the joyful, exciting, wonder-filled moments give way to the routine cycle of ordinary life and work. Time passed quietly in Bethlehem. The glories of Christmas night faded into the grey light of midwinter mornings. For Mary, Joseph, and the child life slowly assumed more tranquil ways. The people of Roman-occupied Palestine continued their daily tasks, unaware that on one splendid night angels sang in the skies above Judea, heralding the birth of the long-awaited Savior.

Just a few weeks after that great choir had sung his praise, the Son of God slept peacefully in the cradle of his mother's arms, rocked in the slow sway of the donkey carrying them on the short journey from Bethlehem to Jerusalem. The time had come for "their purification according to the law of Moses." Mary and Joseph therefore brought Jesus up to the Holy City "to present him to the Lord" (Luke 2:22).

Countless devout Israelites made the same journey year after year. Their destination was the Temple of the Lord, the magnificent structure rising high on a rocky outcropping and shining in golden splendor before the awed gaze of pilgrims and travelers approaching the city. This was the holy place where the glory of God had dwelled within the gold and marble sanctuary, the Holy of Holies.

To the ancient world the Temple was an architectural wonder. To devout Jews it was the heart of all that was most sacred and meaningful in Israel. The Temple held the center of worship, prayer, sacrifice, and celebration before the Lord of hosts, the Holy One of Israel.

> How lovely is thy dwelling place,
>   O Lord of hosts!
> My soul longs, indeed it faints
>   for the courts of the Lord;
> my heart and my flesh sing for joy
>   to the living God.
>
> Psalm 84:1-2

Daily great throngs of men, women, and children passed in and out of the vast Temple courtyard, the Court of Gentiles. Worshippers bargained with moneychangers and the men who sold animals for Temple sacrifices. Rabbis taught their disciples in sheltered sections of the porticos, and Pharisees discussed the Law. Within its walls people prayed, while beggars cried out for alms outside its gates. Roman soldiers and Temple guards were very much in evidence.

Despite the noise, confusion, and marketplace atmosphere of the outer courtyard, the Temple and its sanctuary radiated the holiness of Jewish faith, the Law and tradition. Here, surrounded by the people of the covenant going about their daily business, rested the heritage of Israel: its history of triumph and tragedy, the continuing record of faithful adherence to the covenant, periods of treachery and betrayal. Here was the center of Jewish learning, beauty, and wisdom, of celebrations and sufferings, fears and always hopes.

In the Temple devout Israelites sang God's praise in psalms that had been part of their religious life for centuries. They brought alms, dropping coins into silver trumpets placed for the purpose around the Court of Women. Here the people made and fulfilled vows, gave thanks to God, offered sacrifice, and atoned for sin. Here too they prayed earnestly for the coming of the Messiah.

Unknown to all in the crowds that midwinter day and almost unnoticed, Mary and Joseph entered the courtyard with the baby Jesus. Once inside the Temple the young couple arranged to sacrifice "a pair of turtledoves or two young pigeons" (Luke 2:24), the offering of poor people, to complete the ritual purification of the mother forty days following childbirth. And thus it happened: as they passed through the great gates of the Temple's inner courts, they brought God's Son into his Father's house.

Still too new in life and too tiny to be aware of his surroundings, the baby stirred and then slept on serenely through the turmoil. The crowds that milled around the family were as unconscious of the event as he was. Yet they had received an unexpected gift: the longed-for Messiah had come to his Temple; the Holy One had entered his holy place, as the prophets foretold:

> And the Lord whom you seek will suddenly come to his temple. The messenger of the covenant in whom you delight—indeed, he is coming, says the Lord of hosts.
>
> Malachi 3:1

Where the glory of God had dwelled in the sanctuary of gold, the Son of God entered as a little child, one of the least of his people. Jesus came into his Temple as one "born of a woman, born under the law" (Gal 4:4), like us in all things but sin.

The Holy Family might have completed their worship without attracting notice from the people who prayed around them but for the work of the Holy Spirit. The Spirit had overshadowed Mary at the incarnation, and then had revealed the presence of the Lord within her to the unborn John and to his mother, Elizabeth. Now the Spirit prompted a devout, righteous man named Simeon to come that day from his home in Jerusalem to the Temple, there to meet Mary and Joseph when they "came to do for Jesus what was customary under the law" (Luke 2:27).

The man who came through the Temple gate and crossed the courtyard pavement with firm strides was one whose faith was as strong and sure as the rocky mount on which the Temple stood. Simeon's trust was in the Lord. He looked with confidence for the consolation of Israel. By the revelation of the Spirit he knew he "would not see death before he had seen the Lord's Messiah" (v. 26). Simeon may have been nearing the end of his days on earth, but the hope that filled him gave strength to his heart, vigor to his movements, youthful brightness to his eyes.

Simeon walked directly to Mary, paused at her side, and looked at the child. Then, taking Jesus up in his arms, he blessed God:

> Master, now you are dismissing
>   your servant in peace,
> according to your word;
> for my eyes have seen your salvation,
>   which you have prepared in the presence
>   of all peoples,
> a light for revelation to the Gentiles
>   and for glory to your people Israel.
>   Luke 2:29-32

This dynamic man of firm faith, confidently open to the promptings of the Holy Spirit, knew the child he held close to his great heart was the Anointed One of God, the bearer of light and peace. He was not surprised that the messianic Savior entered the world in a weak and lowly state.

Simeon saw the glory of God in the baby Jesus as clearly as the shepherds had seen the same glory shining around the angel choirs above the fields of Bethlehem. Here was the salvation made ready in the sight of all peoples, from the devout Israelites in the courtyard that morning to the Gentiles who would come streaming "to the mountain of the Lord, to the house of the God of Jacob; that he may teach us his ways and that we may walk in his paths" (Isa 2:3).

Simeon comes to us through Luke's story as a person who entrusted himself to God, one who sang with the psalmist:

> For God alone my soul waits in silence;
> >for my hope is from him.
> He only is my rock and my salvation,
> >my fortress; I shall not be shaken.
> >>>>>>>>>Psalm 62:5-6

He stood for all of God's people. Like Mary he represented the *anawim* who knew the Lord as their rock of refuge, their tower of strength against enemies, their shelter in the storm. God was the place where one could take a stand; in him life had meaning and destiny. One found a home, as it were, a rock on which to build a house and firm ground for living. Like Moses before him, Simeon grounded his life in the God who said:

> I AM WHO I AM. This is my name forever, and this my title for all generations.
> >>>>>>>>>Exodus 3:14,15

The God with whom Simeon took his stand was steadfast in kindness and love, firm and solid like the rock of the Temple mount. He was more than that. Earthly rock can crumble and fall. The very support on which one depended can become an instrument of destruction, just as mountains can fall into valleys and stone tumble into the sea.

God never changed. His faithfulness endured; his covenant once made stood for all time, even when his people time and again rejected him, turned from his ways, and betrayed him. An old hymn sings:

> If thou but suffer God to guide thee,
> And hope in him through all thy ways,
> He'll give thee strength what-e'er betide thee,
> And bear thee through the evil days;
> Who trusts in God's unchanging love
> Builds on a rock that naught can move.[1]

All this Simeon knew with all the strength of his rock-like faith, as he held Jesus and spoke with his surprised parents. For the child he foresaw a continuing pattern of betrayal and rejection. Indeed, Malachi's prophecy had asked, "But who can endure the day of his coming and who can stand when he appears?" (3:2).

Simeon turned to the mother:

> This child is destined for the falling and the rising of many in Israel, and to be a sign that will be opposed so that the inner thoughts of many will be revealed.
> Luke 2:34,35

He spoke of God's Son as one might speak of a stone set in place for the foundation of a building. In the child he saw the "foundation stone, a tested stone, a precious cornerstone, a sure foundation," Isaiah had prophesied the Lord of hosts would "lay in Zion" (28:16). But the cornerstone also would be a "rock one stumbles over—a trap and a snare for the inhabitants of Jerusalem" (8:14). The foundation stone set by the Lord would be rejected by the builders, both houses of Israel as well as the inhabitants of Jerusalem. (See 1 Pet 2:6-8.) The contemporary architects of Jewish faith, the men who were best prepared to welcome the Messiah, would fail to recognize in Jesus of Nazareth the Holy One of God. Most of the learned scribes, devout priests, and knowledgeable Pharisees would oppose him, and in the end reject him even as Jesus himself challenged them:

> Have you not read this scripture:
> "The stone that the builders rejected
>   has become the cornerstone;
> this was the Lord's doing,
>   and it is amazing in our eyes"?
>
> Mark 12:10

In Jesus God's steadfast love became manifest, his Word became flesh, his Truth entered our history. He came among his own people with no fanfare, no command, no easy promises; he simply offered himself to be the world's salvation, to bring new life to everyone. He entered our world a helpless infant, dependent for his existence on the care of Mary and Joseph. Nothing is as powerless as a newly born creature, and human babies remain almost helpless for many months.

The weakness and helplessness of the infant would be mirrored years later in the condemned man held powerless, nailed to a cross set on a rocky hill outside Jerusalem. Eternal love was embodied in the baby boy Simeon cradled in his arms, and shone forth in the passion of the Lord Jesus who steadfastly fulfilled the work his Father asked him to do.

During his lifetime few among his people knew who Jesus was. His fellow townspeople took offense at his wisdom and mighty works, simply because they could not grasp where a man who was one of them could "get all this" (Mark 6:2). The Pharisees refused to accept the signs and wonders he worked because, among other reasons, "we do not know where he comes from" (John 9:29). The chief priests insisted that "no prophet is to arise from Galilee" (7:52). In their blindness they stumbled against the precious chosen cornerstone set for judgment of the many who rejected God's word and thus fell by their own choice.

The startled mother who marveled at Simeon's words and blessing was among the people who were as open to receive God's offer of salvation as Simeon was. Mary herself was blessed, because she "believed that there would be a fulfillment of what was spoken to her by the Lord" (Luke 1:45). Such faith is God's gift, but one must sustain it. Simeon foresaw the difficulties ahead, for he told Mary in an aside, "A sword will pierce through your own soul too" (2:35).

Mary knew the sometimes piercing anguish of making choices and decisions as her son grew to manhood. She was aware early that his mission must consume his time and energy, that the good news of the kingdom came first, and that her relationship to Jesus must transcend the demands of family ties and embrace all whom he counted as his brothers, sisters, and mother.

In the days when Simeon's prophecy became reality in the life of Jesus, when the thoughts of many hearts revealed opposition and hatred for him, Mary must have experienced her own struggles. Sorrow and concern indeed thrust like swords, for she was the mother seeing the mockery, hearing the scoffs and the threats directed against her beloved son. She knew the pain of separation and realized sadly that the child she had borne belonged to others.

And finally her son was destroyed, executed as a criminal, accursed under the Law of her people and her faith. Here was another stumbling block, as Paul would write later to his congregation in Corinth:

> We proclaim Christ crucified, a stumbling block to Jews and foolishness to Gentiles, but to those who are the called, both Jews and Greeks, Christ the power of God and the wisdom of God.
> 1 Corinthians 1:23-24

Mary, once called by God, remained faithful, following her son even to the cross. While she may have experienced doubts and sometimes failed to understand what her son was about, she neither dismissed nor sought to avoid the realities of his life and ministry. Her faith, like Simeon's, was founded on the rock of God's word to his people.

All disciples of the Lord encounter difficulties and struggle with doubts as they strive to live the paradoxes of Christian faith: wisdom in folly, strength in weakness, life in death. All disciples experience the thrusting power of God's Word, forcing them to make a choice, God's way or the way of the world.

> Indeed, the word of God is living and active, sharper than any two-edged sword, piercing until it divides soul from spirit, joints from marrow; it is able to judge the thoughts and intentions of the heart.
>
> Hebrews 4:12

All face the possibility of stumbling and coming to grief in the blindness of a choice that turns them from following the path leading to life.

The gift of faith is the strongest support for those who receive the Lord into their hearts and lives. Mary, Joseph, and Simeon were people of faith, who put their trust in the steadfast love of God. Together they became part of the foundation, the living stones of Israel's faith on which the new covenant would be established.

Mary and Joseph had come to the Temple simply to fulfill the requirements of the Law. They encountered there the man who, prompted by the Holy Spirit, joyfully and exultantly confirmed what they knew of the child they consecrated to God. They also heard the ominous warnings of what that consecration would mean for his life and for theirs.

Mary was one who pondered the events of her son's life in her heart. Surely this meeting with Simeon added to her motherly concern even as it prepared her for her own dedication to the way of the kingdom and her role as a disciple of the Lord.

The ominous tones of Simeon's warning may have been eased at least for a time by the appearance of a devout daughter of Abraham, who also recognized in the infant Jesus the Holy One of God, the Messiah promised to Israel. She was the prophetess Anna who was always in the Temple, worshipping God, fasting, and praying night and day. Coming up to the small group just as Simeon finished speaking, she began to cry out praise to God, and "to speak about the child to all who were looking for the redemption of Jerusalem" (Luke 2:38).

A few weeks after his birth and within the great Jerusalem Temple founded on rock, Jesus began to reveal himself to his people as the true Temple, the place where God's glory abides. Here in faith an old man and an old woman received the revelation of the Spirit with joy and went forth in the knowledge that God had fulfilled his promise by sending his own Son to be the Savior, Redeemer, and Messiah of Israel. To most observers in the Temple that day Jesus was just another baby, but Simeon and Anna saw with the eyes of faith beyond the apparent insignificance and weakness, and gave their lives into his tiny hands.

All that was splendid in Israel gathered that midwinter morning beneath the great columns of the Temple; the Law, the Prophets, the faithful sons and daughters of Abraham met in the Spirit around the baby Jesus. The old age prepared to depart in peace, for the new age had dawned.

The memory of Simeon, that stout old man of faith, reverently and joyfully embracing the Lord's Anointed in his Temple has symbolized for generations the fulfilled longing of an ancient people for regeneration, renewal, and the life only God can give. Simeon, the devout, obedient, faithful Israelite took his stand on the high rock wall of God's faithful love. He waited for the Lord as the watchman waits on the wall of his city, searching the horizon, longing for the dawn of the new day.

For Simeon the final blessing of God came with the baby Jesus into the Temple. Giving the child back to his mother, he turned away from the little group. With firm strides he crossed the courtyard and passed through the great gates of the Temple for the last time. His eyes had seen the salvation of God. Within his great heart shone the light of revelation and of glory, scattering the darkness and shadow of earthly existence. Dawn had come. Simeon's watch was over. The long night of waiting had ended.

NOTE

1. Georg Neumark, trans. Catherine Winkworth, in *The Book of Hymns* (Nashville: The Methodist Publishing House, © 1960, 1964) No. 210.

Finding Jesus in the Temple

I Must Be in My Father's House
Luke 2:49

Nazareth, the isolated, inconsequential town to which Joseph brought his family after their return to Galilee, has attracted and inspired Christians in every age. While some contemporaries may have shared Nathaniel's disdain for the place, later disciples of Jesus found in the image of Nazareth the basis for a rich, dynamic spirituality. For them Nazareth symbolized a way of life that drew them close to the Lord on a deeply meaningful, human level.

In Nazareth we meet our Lord at home in our world. The Incarnate Son of God came into this setting as a very small, dependent child. He grew, as we all grow, to adulthood, perhaps, as one evangelist observed, to a fuller, more complete maturity than most of us.

> The child grew and became strong, filled with wisdom;
> and the favor of God was upon him.
> Luke 2:40

In Nazareth were laid the foundations of Jesus' life and ministry. The love and example of his parents, the wisdom of his teachers, the company of friends and relatives, all these boyhood experiences bore fruit in the man who later left his home to preach the gospel of his Father's kingdom, to confront the opposition and hostility of religious leaders in his day, and finally to give his life on the cross.

The evangelists write almost nothing of Jesus' childhood and youth. The record of his public life and preaching, however, makes one aware of the richness, breadth, and depth of those formative years. The reader quickly appreciates the profound influence of our Lord's early surroundings.

One readily can imagine the boy Jesus exploring the fields near his home, delighting in the beauty of flowers blooming in the warm spring sunshine, fascinated by the birds wheeling and swooping across the bright skies. This little boy knew the shepherds who tended the sheep and goats belonging to the townspeople; he spent some of his days watching the flocks with them in the hills above the town.

The caravans crossing the plains of Esdraelon below Nazareth opened his eyes and his mind to the world that lay beyond the familiar center of his home. Roman legions marching along the same roads and the ever-present tax collectors in the marketplace taught the boy that his was a subject nation, a people dominated by foreign power.

Year after year Jesus must have helped plant seeds in the family garden, and rejoiced with his parents when conditions favored the growth of the new wheat and its slow ripening under the hot sun toward harvest. He wondered at the gnarled ancient trees spreading patches of cool shade and at the tiny seeds borne on puffs of wind to fall into hospitable soil and sprout new growth.

Under the watchful training of Joseph the boy learned carpentry, the discipline of a craft, and the value of work. His small hands grew as the years passed, becoming more sensitive and skilled in shaping the wood.

From an early age, as his preaching and his confrontations with religious authorities would make clear, Jesus was steeped in the heritage of Israel. The life and practice of his devout, faithful parents taught him reverence and respect for the Temple and its religious significance. His own love for God developed and found expression in prayer, praise, and thanksgiving. In the synagogue with other boys he learned to read the scrolls of the Law and the Prophets, to ponder and discuss the wisdom they contained. On Sabbath days he joined in worship, taking part in the liturgy and the singing of psalms. "In this way, the human feelings, the dispositions of heart and will, by means of which Jesus effected our salvation had gradually been formed in His experience as a young Jew and in His education at Nazareth by Mary and Joseph."[1]

The Gospels record a single incident from Jesus' boyhood. It suggests that the years of growing and learning in Nazareth already were bearing fruit. For Luke who tells it, the story offers a sign of the boy's destiny, a point along the continuum of his life arcing from the moment of his conception to the supreme hour of his passion and death on the cross.

During the boy's twelfth year Mary and Joseph, taking Jesus with them, went up to Jerusalem, to celebrate the annual pilgrimage festival of Passover, the solemn celebration of Israel's release from bondage in Egypt. Probably this was not the boy's first journey from Nazareth to the Holy City, the center of Jewish faith and worship. No doubt he had been in the Temple itself several times since his presentation there.

In his twelfth year, however, Jesus was old enough to assume some adult responsibilities. He could leave his mother in the Court of Women, and enter with Joseph and other adult male Jews into the Court of Israel. For the first time the boy would be an active participant in fulfilling the commands of the Lord for keeping the Passover. Jesus must have been an eager young pilgrim in the family caravan making its way from Galilee up to Jerusalem.

Participating in the Temple ritual and worship during that Passover celebration evidently had a profound effect on Jesus. He spent much of his time in the Temple. His curiosity led him to the groups gathered around the rabbis and doctors of the Law as they instructed their disciples under the porticos in the immense courtyard of the Temple.

At first perhaps he stood on the fringe of things, but soon his eagerness to hear and be a part of everything drew him into various groups, where he became absorbed in listening to the wise men and then asking them questions. Jesus must have been excellent company even as a boy, for he provoked interest among the rabbis who were amazed at the depth of his understanding. It never occurred to him that the festival had ended, that the time had come for the return to Nazareth. Jesus was too wrapped up in the feast of heart and mind, that kept him in the Temple absorbing all he could about the God of Israel.

For Mary and Joseph the celebration was over; duties at home required their return to Nazareth. Assuming that Jesus was somewhere among the relatives and friends traveling in caravan back to Galilee, they began the journey without concern over the fact that he was not actually with them. It was not until the next morning that they realized he was missing. Immediately they returned to Jerusalem. The search consumed another anxious day. On the third day they found him in what to them was an unlikely place, the Temple. Both parents were astonished when they saw the boy talking with the rabbis and heard him asking them questions.

Mary's reaction echoed the cry of concerned mothers and fathers in any age. Her relief at finding her child, combined with the anxiety and fear of the past few days, burst forth in her rebuke, "Child, why have you treated us like this? Look, your father and I have been searching for you in great anxiety" (Luke 2:48).

Even more astonishing was Jesus' response to his parents' concern; he could not imagine why they did not know where he would be. "Why were you searching for me? Did you not know that I must be in my Father's house?" (v. 49).

Jesus like many twelve-year-olds stood on the brink of adult independence and responsibilities. His mind was opening to new ideas, new ways of thought, new experiences. In his eagerness the boy sought to learn as much as possible, to understand his religious and cultural heritage. He had begun to experience a deeper relationship with the God of his fathers.

During the Passover celebration he had been close for the first time to the great altar of sacrifice and the shining golden sanctuary of the Temple, the holiest place on earth. He stood before the sanctuary of the God who had spoken to Moses out of the burning bush and revealed his name, I AM.

The God of Israel had brought his people from slavery in Egypt to freedom in the Promised Land. He had led them along the way, rescued them from certain disaster by parting the Red Sea waters and thus allowing them to escape the Egyptian forces pursuing them. He had marched with them through the desert, in the pillar of cloud by day and the column of fire by night.

The spirit of God, the *Shekinah*, had descended within the sanctuary of the Temple, to rest above the cherubim protecting the Ark of the Covenant and the tablets of the Law given by God to Moses on Mount Sinai centuries before. The Temple enshrined all that meant life to Israel, the enduring covenant with the Lord of hosts, the God of Abraham, Isaac, and Jacob, of David and Solomon.

In this awesome setting Jesus realized a far deeper, more profound relationship with God. The experience must have been almost overwhelming. It is no wonder he felt there was only one place for him in Jerusalem, in his Father's house, concerned with the things of his Father.

The experience of Jesus in the Temple is not unlike that of many young people through the centuries. Countless

Christians trace their faith back to the foundation of a believing family, a trusting childhood relationship with God, and a dynamic love that held each family member in esteem under all circumstances.

Youngsters often are radiantly open to the possibilities God offers them. The experience of a suddenly deeper encounter with the Lord remains the basis for subsequent meetings and supports one through the difficulties life holds for everyone. John Paul II recalled such an experience, one that took place when he was "still a youngster" in the Cathedral of Cracow during a solemn liturgy of Holy Week.

> To this day I often think back to that, because the experience was quite unique; it has never returned with the same intensity, even in the same cathedral, during similar celebrations. It was not merely discovery of the beauty and spiritual attractiveness of the Holy Week liturgy; it was above all discovery of the dimension of the absolute, of the mystery expressed in the liturgy and which the liturgy conveys as a message that is valid for all time.[2]

Such an experience holds deep meaning for a young person, but it often surprises parents. Mary and Joseph reacted in astonishment. They simply did not understand what the boy was saying. In a sense, Jesus suddenly had grown beyond the child they brought to Jerusalem. His leap beyond the family circle into his own destiny stunned them. In the Temple Jesus' identity was revealed once again, but this time it was the boy himself who proclaimed it.

The idea was not easy to grasp. Jesus' own circle of followers and friends as well as disciples in every age of Christianity have had trouble comprehending who Jesus really is. For Mary and Joseph the boy's revelation was wrapped in mystery, and for a time they were left standing outside it.

Jesus also seemed surprised. His reply to Mary hints of some disappointment. He expected his parents to realize that he could be found only in the Temple. Where else would he go?

There is a dimension in the incident, that goes beyond a youngster's eager involvement in a moment of ineffable understanding. The boy's words to his mother, "I must be in my Father's house," convey a sense of Jesus' response to God, a response that meant doing what the Father asked of him. He was obedient to the will of God, as if he seemed already to know that his relationship with his Father, his fulfillment of the Father's will, transcended family ties and earthly relationships. This early understanding apparently permeated his life immediately, for Luke tells us that Jesus obeyed the will of God in fulfilling the commandments of the Law.

> Then he went down with them and came to Nazareth, and was obedient to them.
> Luke 2:51

The early education in Nazareth already was bearing fruit. Home and family helped to form the human consciousness and shape the religious attitudes of God's Son.

In this single incident of Jesus' youth we encounter the One who is Lord and Redeemer, the Messiah of God. With Mary and Joseph we approach the awesome mystery of the incarnation, manifested in the relationship between the God of Israel and the boy from Nazareth, between the eternal Father and his Son, the Second Person of the Trinity. Jesus the Son knew his Father in the infinite depths of Divine Being, far beyond the limits of the human mind and heart. Yet the Incarnate Son experienced and expressed this relationship through the mind and heart of a twelve-year-old boy.

Late twentieth-century Christians would speak of an *Abba* experience, a meeting with our Father-God, that seems to lift us from our current stream of existence, propelling our life into new and more demanding channels. It is a moment when we come "to know him through the realization that our very being is penetrated with his knowledge and love for us."³

This is divine wisdom, the gift of God's merciful love for his people. It is a wisdom "we see in a mirror, dimly" (1 Cor 13:12). For the Incarnate Lord, "the image of the invisible God" (Col 1:15), such wisdom came to a human mind illumined by his own eternal presence as Son to his Father. Christ is the eternal Word of the Father, of the God who is Truth itself.

Jesus, like us in all things but sin, grew in wisdom and grace. As God's Son he also experienced the infinite love and truth of the Father through the Holy Spirit who accompanied him throughout his life. Enlightened in the infinite wisdom of his Sonship, Jesus came to understand that his destiny transcended the messianic expectations of the Israelites in his day, that the kingdom of God encompassed infinitely more than the earthly kingdom his compatriots longed to see established. He was King of Kings and Lord of Lords, but in the Temple a twelve-year-old boy proclaimed himself the obedient Son of his heavenly Father. Through such obedience he would bring about the salvation of the Father's world.

Human understanding falters here; all analogies are simply meaningless before the mystery of God's Incarnate Word. The Son, although he was eternally divine, plunged himself so deeply into our limiting human experience and the daily realities of earthly life that Luke recorded simply, "And Jesus increased in wisdom and in years, and in divine and human favor" (Luke 2:51).

Our Lord was faithful to the Father he encountered in the Jerusalem Temple and continued to meet in prayer throughout his life. He was faithful as well to the teaching of his parents, to his early training in Nazareth, in brief, to his heritage as a son of Abraham. The obedience he gave to Mary and Joseph during those years was the foundation of the obedience he offered to his Father in Gethsemane and on the cross: "Father, not my will but yours be done" (Luke 22:42).

Jesus' obedience is a temporal image of the eternal obedience he offered as Son to his Father. It is obvious that, "Although he was a Son, he learned obedience" not only "through what he suffered," as the author of Hebrews points out (5:8), but also through living the commandment of God to Israel:

> Honor your father and your mother, so that your days may be long in the land that the Lord your God is giving you.
> Exodus 20:12

If Jesus himself had to learn, had to grow to maturity, how much more must we be aware of our own clouded understanding concerning our ways before God and our journey toward the fullness of life he offers us. Mary and Joseph were mystified by the boy's response when after an anxious search they found him in the Temple. While their reaction to his coolness is one with which most parents readily identify, it is also symbolic of our limited human ability to see and hear our infinite, transcendent God.

On our own we do not know who Jesus is. We recognize him because God grants us the grace that clears our eyes and opens our ears. This gift is faith, eternally offered to his people. We have only to remain open as Jesus was to the divine presence that never departs from us, never lets us go.

For Mary who "treasured all these things in her heart" (Luke 2:51), vision and hearing, graced with the light of faith, became clearer in time. The frightening, painful experience of losing and then finding her child was the first shadow of the sword that would pierce her heart. In her the obedience of faith, "Let it be with me according to your word," never faltered, even when the rejection and suffering of her son anguished her own heart.

From this incident of Jesus' youth Mary too learned something of the demands obedience would make of her. Circumstances forced her beyond the wrenching struggle most mothers experience as their children grow and mature away from the family center, as they encounter the realities of a harsh world. Mary gave her son to a way of life and a mission she did not always understand, but she continued to reflect on the events of his life, pondering them in her heart.

Mary's obedience of faith is like that of a disciple hearing again and again the Word of the Lord and each time keeping it. This is the obedience to which every Christian is called, for we must be open to receive our God and Father as he reveals himself to us, not as we want him to be. We accept certain aspects of our faith without insisting on complete understanding. We are ready to learn; we allow faith to grow, remembering that now God speaks to us through his Son.

Like Mary we treasure all these things, these mysteries of our faith, in our hearts where we may know God, the ground and source of our being, in Christ his Son. With an early disciple we believe that, "The grace of our Lord overflowed for me with the faith and love that are in Christ Jesus" (1 Tim 1:14).

With Mary his mother we ponder in faith the mysteries of Jesus' life and mission at home in our own Nazareth. Then we set off to follow him on his journey, to stand beneath his cross in our own lives, and to wait with his disciples for his Spirit to descend and lead us where he will.

NOTES

1. Yves Congar, O.P., *Jesus Christ*, trans. Luke O'Neill (New York: Herder and Herder, 1966) 55.

2. Karol Woytyla (Pope John Paul II), *Sign of Contradiction*, trans. St. Paul Publications (New York: The Seabury Press, 1979) 82.

3. Thomas Merton, *Contemplative Prayer* (New York: Herder and Herder, 1969) 103.

Interlude

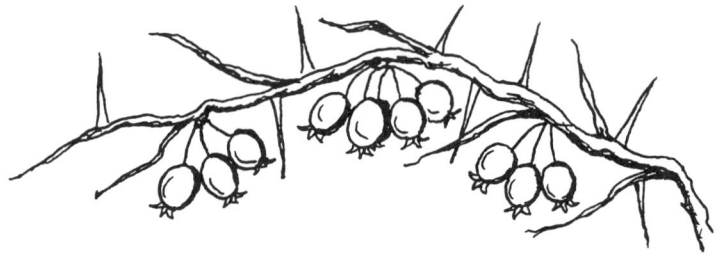

Yours Is the Kingdom of God
Luke 6:20

God sent his Son into our world to proclaim a message of joy and hope to all people of good will. At the heart of this good news lies promise and opportunity. The Son's gospel preaches the reign of God, the wonderful truth that "in fact, the kingdom of God is in the midst of you" (Luke 17:21). For Jesus of Nazareth, God is Lord and ruler of history. He spent his life trying to make that reality clear to everyone.

Jesus proclaimed that to be truly human, to become who we really are, whole and perfect as God intended us to be from the beginning, we must turn to the Lord and enter into relationship with him. In essence this is the way the New Testament understands the kingdom: it is a relationship, a covenant, in which God, source of being for all of creation, is the dominant or sovereign member.

The offer of relationship and covenant with the Lord is his gift to us. When we receive it, we receive salvation as long as we also receive God's rule, his commandments and ways, and make them our own. In Jesus God summons us to leave behind the ways of this world bent under the weight of evil, turn away from the sin that separates us from him and sets us at odds with one another, and take on the easy yoke, the light burden of Christ.

This indeed is good news. In Jesus we experience the forgiveness of God and reconciliation with him. We are united within the triune relationship of Father, Son, and Holy Spirit. The promise of the kingdom is no less than salvation for the world, a share in the divine communion of love, joy, and peace.

As Christians we live and work that God's reign will become reality in the hearts of all men and women.

> You are a chosen race, a royal priesthood, a holy nation, God's own people, in order that you may proclaim the mighty acts of him who called you out of darkness into his marvelous light.
> 1 Peter 2:9

It was to this splendid state that our Lord called the people of Galilee and Judea two thousand years ago. He proclaimed the reign of God to everyone who would listen; he offered its benefits to all who were open to receive them.

The boy who once told his parents, "I must be in my Father's house, concerned with the affairs of my Father," became the prophet and preacher of his Father's kingdom, saying: "I must proclaim the good news of the kingdom of God; for I was sent for this purpose" (Luke 4:43).

The God whose kingdom Jesus preached is hidden; he revealed himself in the gift of his Son to humankind. The reign of God entered human history in the person of Jesus. He *is* the kingdom, because in him God lives and rules. In Jesus God himself speaks to his people not as a being remote from them, bound in his eternity, but as a loving, merciful Father who cares for them and longs to be with them.

Jesus embodied God's love and peace, gathering all our sinning to himself and mercifully triumphing over it. He embodied as well the most perfect human response to the

Father's offer of salvation. Because God lives and reigns in him, Jesus of Nazareth shows us the path to life and fullness of joy in his presence (see Ps 16:11).

God's Son accepted his Father's mission in loving obedience and remained faithful to it. In the power of God's Spirit the Word became flesh. He received the Spirit at his baptism in the Jordan River. Driven by the Spirit he journeyed into the wilderness of Judea, encountered and overcame the temptation of Satan to use magic and earthly power to fulfill the task that lay before him. In the power of the Spirit he returned to Galilee to proclaim God's message. Truly God was with his Son.

As opposition and hostility toward him increased, Jesus drew closer to his Father, spending whole nights in prayer. Through the tumult of his public ministry he remained in the Father he loved and served, saying: "The Father is in me and I am in the Father" (John 10:38).

Jesus' life expressed confident joy in his vision of God's kingdom. His reign would bring light to triumph over darkness, truth and justice to hold sway in human hearts, and the victory of goodness over the forces of sin and death. He saw his Father's world aflame with the fire of a new creation, new possibilities, new hope.

The kingdom comes from the infinite God to finite human beings, created in his image and likeness, but limited in their vision and understanding, and always free to choose the path they will follow in the life given them. Jesus and his disciples after him preached "what God has prepared for those who love him." They proclaimed, as St. Paul wrote, "God's wisdom, secret and hidden, which God decreed before the ages for our glory" (1 Cor 2:7). Such wisdom "no eye has seen, nor ear heard, nor the heart of man conceived" (v. 9).

Jesus taught his followers through parables. The very ambiguity of his stories meant that his hearers would have to make their choice to receive or reject the kingdom, not under constraint but freely. He told the disciples who questioned his practice of speaking to the crowd in parables, "To you it has been given to know the secrets of the kingdom, but to them it has not been given" (Matt 13:11). Those who refused to hear and see fulfilled the prophecy:

> This people's heart has grown dull,
>   and their ears are hard of hearing,
>   and they have shut their eyes;
> so that they might not look with their eyes,
>   and listen with their ears,
> and understand with their heart
>   and turn—
> and I would heal them.
> Matthew 13:15

It is not easy to enter the kingdom of God. Riches of a material nature constitute one barrier, not because wealth is necessarily wrong or intrinsically evil, but because the person who has enough and to spare of this world's goods is likely to be complacent, satisfied, unaware of the serious importance of heeding the message of God's reign. The heart of one who is complacent is dull.

But the heart of one who recognizes personal limitations and poverty is far more honest. It recognizes its burden of sin, its need for the mercy God offers. Such a heart is open, to be filled with the Word of the Lord.

Centuries before the Deuteronomist commented, "You will seek the Lord your God, and you will find him if you search after him with all your heart and soul" (4:29). To the little ones who seek him, God gives the wisdom that enables men and women to see and hear the hidden things of God, the mysteries of the kingdom. Jesus described these people many times as he spoke to the crowds who flocked to him. The poor in spirit, the singlehearted, the hungry, meek, oppressed, and persecuted of this world received his Word as seed sown in hearts longing for all that creation promises to humankind, all God offers his people in Christ Jesus. Perhaps the Beatitudes Jesus taught his disciples on the mountain might be summed up, "Blessed are those who know their need of God and turn to him wholeheartedly."

The kingdom Jesus proclaimed is compassion, tenderness, and mercy. It radiates not power and pomp but a passionate concern for people in need. Jesus is Emmanuel; he is with us to the very depths of all that is human about us. In him God reached out to everyone, saint and sinner alike, but his tenderest care was for the poor and the oppressed. He welcomed the sinner, the outcast, the prisoner, saying, "I have come to call not the righteous, but sinners to repentance" (Luke 5:32). No one stood beyond his healing embrace.

The coming of the kingdom means that the last word is not with the sinner, nor is it with the complacent and self-righteous; it is with God who in his loving mercy grants forgiveness to all who turn to him. Jesus preached the good news to the poor and to the sinners of his day, to the *anawim* who knew their need of healing. Reading from the scroll of the prophet Isaiah in the synagogue at Nazareth he declared:

> The Spirit of the Lord is upon me,
> because he has anointed me to bring
>   good news to the poor.
> He has sent me to proclaim release
>   to the captives
> and recovery of sight to the blind,
> to let the oppressed go free,
> to proclaim the year of the Lord's favor.
>   Luke 4:18-19

Then he sat down and said, "Today this scripture has been fulfilled in your hearing" (v. 21).

The kingdom has drawn very near to all peoples in Jesus; but the reign of God in all its fullness is still to come. It is established "on earth as it is in heaven" (Matt 6:10) only when men and women wholeheartedly receive it, place themselves under its rule, and accept its obligation to proclaim the gospel in and through their own lives.

Jesus heard the word of the kingdom perfectly. Obedient to his Father's will, he refused to compromise his mission and the Father he revealed to his people as truth, love, justice, and mercy. He proclaimed and lived the message of God in our world, the setting in which he is alive and active today.

We as Christians are called to be active where God in his Son works to reconcile the world to himself. God's people do not wait for the kingdom; they have come into his vineyard to work. To the extent that we receive the Word and allow him to be present and active within us, to that extent God's kingdom is real and present.

Living within the kingdom places demands upon each Christian just as it placed demands upon our Lord. Jesus alone in the Judean wilderness confronted temptations to choose an easy way, to pursue earthly power. As his ministry advanced, opposition to him became increasingly hostile. People failed to understand, dismissed him with charges of blasphemy, drunkenness, gluttony, consorting with sinners.

To stand before the world as his Father asked, with the truth, love, and mercy of God as his message, meant that Jesus also stood before the freedom of people to receive it. Acceptance requires a radical reordering of priorities, a conversion that turns one's life around. One who receives the reign of God believes *into Christ*, as the Greek of John's Gospel puts it. One accepts Jesus as the bearer of the kingdom, accepts the truth of his word about its priorities and his commandments concerning love for God and neighbor.

Many in Israel rejected the good news, rejected Jesus' preference for the poor and oppressed, rejected his word concerning the Law of God, rejected him. Within a short time the teacher from Galilee became notorious in official

Jerusalem. Eventually branded as an outlaw, Jesus had to take refuge in the wilderness with his disciples. When he came to the Holy City, only the enthusiasm and adulation of the crowds gathered to celebrate the Passover saved him from immediate arrest. In the end Jesus stood a failure, rejected by men who sought to destroy him utterly.

Our Lord preached the good news of salvation to all; but not everyone will receive it, nor will they turn from the sinful ways of this world to accept God's gentle yoke. Each person is free to reject the gospel and accept the consequences.

As long as people choose to operate under the cover of darkness, the light of God's kingdom cannot illumine our world completely. The reign of God also constitutes his judgment of the world and its history, and the kingdom is still to come. As Jesus told Pilate, "My kingdom is not from this world" (John 18:36).

Yet he knew the reign of God would become a reality as surely as the tiny mustard seed, hidden and growing in the soil, produces a great tree whose branches give shelter to the birds of the air. He foresaw a day and an hour when the sign of the Son of man would appear in heaven, and all the tribes of the earth would "see the Son of man coming on the clouds of heaven with power and great glory" (Matt 24:30). Then God will establish his reign, and "the righteous will shine like the sun in the kingdom of their Father" (13:43).

In the Sorrowful Mysteries of the rosary we encounter the dawning kingdom of God in Jesus of Nazareth whose preaching evoked such disparate responses. His fellow townspeople wondered, "Where did the man get all this? What is this wisdom that has been given to him?" And they took offense at him. (See Mark 6:2, 3.) The chief priests, scribes, and elders in Jerusalem debated, "What are we to do? If we let him go on thus, everyone will believe in him, and the Romans will come and destroy both our holy place and our nation" (John 11:47, 48).

Interlude: Yours Is the Kingdom of God

The Temple police reported their excuse for failing to arrest Jesus, "Never has anyone spoken like this!" (7:46). Peter confessed, "You are the Messiah, the Son of the living God" (Matt 16:16). And Martha, his beloved friend, knew, "Yes, Lord; I believe that you are the Messiah, the Son of God, the one coming into the world" (John 11:27).

The motley crowd of disciples and friends gathered around Jesus knew him as their Master and as the man who "went about doing good and healing all that were oppressed by the devil, for God was with him" (Acts 10:38). Many of these people were the outcasts and rejects of their time and place; they counted for very little. Jesus' gift to them was acceptance. In him they experienced healing and knew themselves to be endowed with the dignity of human persons made in the image and likeness of God.

The power of Jesus' personality and preaching called forth the goodness of the little ones who received him. To him they were special. He offered them a vision of a world shining with truth and justice, radiant in fulfilling all the noblest longings of human hearts.

The poor were the first to discover the richness of life in the kingdom of God. Those who were last became the first. They were the first to become disciples, the first to give up everything, to risk possessions, property, even life for the Lord they loved. They were among the first to suffer persecution and martyrdom, the first to heed the Master's warning, "Whoever does not carry the cross and follow me cannot be my disciple" (Luke 14:27).

Through all the ages of Christianity the poor and marginalized people of the world have welcomed God's Word, allowing it to enrich their lives and to lift their struggle for existence to a truly noble level. For them the gift of life is precious, and the space and time of their journey on earth is lit by the reign of God in their hearts.

Among these precious human beings to whom the kingdom belongs we find Mary, Jesus' mother, one of the *anawim* who know their need of God. Mary received God's

Word into her heart as she received his Son into her womb. In her loving acceptance of God's will she who was full of grace took on herself the priorities and demands of the kingdom.

Pondering the events of his birth and childhood Mary knew confusion as well as increasing concern for her remarkable son. During his public ministry she experienced the anguish of knowing the fulfillment of old Simeon's prophecy, for Jesus in fact became "a sign that is opposed" (Luke 2:34). She knew fear when her son was threatened with arrest, hunted as an outlaw. She must have realized with some of his friends that Jesus was in serious danger during the days before the Passover celebration in Jerusalem. She remained with him and knew the suffering of a mother who watched her beloved child die in agony on a cross.

The kingdom always is the grace of God in our Lord Jesus Christ. We know, as Mary and the early disciples knew, that the work of the kingdom did not end with the death of its Lord. It must be renewed in every generation, for its fruits are borne in the hearts of believers to give life, to nourish all who are in need, to draw men and women into a new relationship with God and one another.

Each of us spends a lifetime learning slowly, often painfully to live at constantly deepening levels the ways of the kingdom: the Beatitudes and the Sermon on the Mount, the commandment of Jesus to love and to serve especially the poor and oppressed, the refusal to compromise the kingdom or its Lord. To choose the kingdom affects every aspect of life, but it is the kingdom of that peace only God can give.

Through temptation, the darkness of rejection, failure, and indifference those who proclaim the kingdom know the joy of being found in their Lord, sharing the suffering that is often the consequence of doing God's work, the price of the struggle.

In his Son God has reached across the great abyss of sin, that separates humankind from him to draw us by his final Word into the wholeness and holiness of life with him. He calls us to believe and hope in the kingdom of his love and peace through the conflict and dissension of our earthly life. He asks us to manifest its presence in our midst by the way we live its simple precepts.

Our vision of God's reign is often blurred or darkened by the ugly realities of the world in which we live. We are frail and fragile human beings who stumble easily and fall often. But our eyes fixed on the Lord still can see the goodness, the loveliness of his creation even in our own struggling selves.

One of Caryll Houselander's "rhythms" beautifully expresses in images of autumn the hope God's kingdom brings to his people.

> Milky the mist
> lying over our pastures
> and gleaming like pearl.
> It is October now.
> I walk among shadows,
> but shadows even
> are fires:
> lambent flames of leaves
> and yellow flowers
> and the last roses,
> and warmth with beauty
> is flesh and blood
> sacramental and holy
> for all our sinning.
> Though death walks at my heels
> and welcome,
> this is the beginning,
> not the end of my story.
> I walk among shadows,
> O Liege Lord,
> my love,
> Shadows
> of Your bright glory![1]

The kingdom of glory is a new creation. And, "if anyone is in Christ, there is a new creation; everything old has passed away, see, everything has become new!" (2 Cor 5:17). It is a new creation formed of God's loving mercy through the sunlight and shadow of earthly reality toward eternal communion in that kingdom whose unending light is still the glory of God shining in the face of Christ Jesus, his crucified Son.

NOTE

1. Caryll Houselander, quoted in Maisie Ward, *Caryll Houselander: That Divine Eccentric* (Westminster, Md.: Christian Classics, Inc., 1988) 307, 308.

Jesus' Agony in the Garden

My Soul Is Sorrowful Unto Death
Mark 14:34

The setting sun lingered over the high walls and palaces of Jerusalem, and reflected golden splendor from the pinnacles of the Temple. Down in the narrow streets, already shadowed in twilight, people were making their way to family celebrations of the Passover. Jesus of Nazareth with his disciples slipped quietly among them, and unobtrusively entered a certain house. There two of the group had prepared the Passover meal for their Master and his family of followers to share within the Holy City as the Law required.

Planning for the evening suggests that precautions were taken to assure secrecy. Jesus was a hunted man. Even before his triumphant entry into the Holy City a few days earlier, religious authorities had begun planning to put him to death. (See John 11:53.) No longer did they question whether to arrest him or not; their talk now focused on how to do so by stealth, "or there may be a riot among the people" (Mark 14:2). Already, "the chief priests and the Pharisees had given orders that anyone who knew where Jesus was should let them know, so that they might arrest him" (John 11:57).

Within a few days someone responded. One of Jesus' trusted followers stepped forward to betray his Master and friend in exchange for thirty pieces of silver. Like the religious authorities who paid him for his treachery Judas Iscariot could not, or would not, believe even as Jesus pleaded with the crowds in the Temple:

> The light is with you for a little longer. Walk while you have the light, so that the darkness may not overtake you. While you have the light, believe in the light, so that you may become children of light.
>
> John 12:35, 36

And thus it was in secrecy that Jesus gathered his chosen companions around the supper table that last evening. All of the Twelve were there, Simon Peter and Judas, James, John, Andrew, and the rest, reclining, as was the custom at banquets, within the soft glow of lamps around the table. Beyond their circle dark shadows played, but Jesus' love for his own illumined the meal they shared and the night before them.

Jesus said to them: "I have eagerly desired to eat this Passover with you before I suffer; for I tell you, I will not eat it until it is fulfilled in the kingdom of God" (Luke 22:15, 16). He knew this would be the last Passover, the last meal he would share with his friends. Poignancy and a sense of sorrow mingled with hope, and flickered in the golden light around the ritual meal. Yet Jesus' own courage and his command of events swirling about the little company gave the celebration its aura of joy and confidence.

During the last evening the Master's concern was for his disciples. He sought to draw them closer together, closer to him. His trust in the Father pushed back the dark shadows, although he was well aware of his betrayer's quiet departure into the night to inform the authorities where Jesus of Nazareth could be found.

Opposing forces of friendship and betrayal, hope and fear surged around Jesus as he pledged his own life, laying it down in his great love for his friends.

> Then he took a loaf of bread, and when he had given thanks, he broke it and gave it to them, saying, "This is my body which is given for you. Do this in remembrance of me." And he did the same with the cup after supper, saying, "This cup that is poured out for you is the new covenant in my blood."
> Luke 22:19, 20

It was his own body and blood that Jesus offered at the Last Supper, celebrating in sign what he would offer in reality in his passion and death. Through his sacrifice our Lord made his disciples, together with the people who from every land and nation would believe in him, a communion in his Body and Blood. He united all Christians with his offering. The breaking of bread in remembrance of him today makes us one with him, and signifies to the world Christ's fellowship with his own. We who are many are one body, for we all partake of the one bread and the one cup.

At the Last Supper the meaning of Jesus' words and actions eluded the disciples the Lord had just united to himself. Luke records that once again they argued over which of them was to be regarded as the greatest.

The Passover meal concluded as usual with the singing of a hymn, and Jesus descended from the upper room to the street with his remaining disciples. It was night. The men were aware of danger but evidently were not alarmed about the possibility of discovery. The intentions of the missing Judas were known only to Jesus who may have left the house early in order to spare his host trouble. Once again, Master and disciples walked quietly through the dark streets. They left the city, crossed the Kidron Valley, and went up the Mount of Olives into a garden called Gethsemane.

Behind them in the Holy City lamplight beamed through shutters and glowed from roof-top dining rooms where families lingered over their celebration. In the garden of Gethsemane moonlight shone, flicking bits of silver from the new spring leaves into the gently playing shadows of the olive trees. Only a soft wind and a crunch of sandals on twigs and stones interrupted the stillness.

A huge, ominous darkness seemed to settle around Jesus and the disciples. Apprehension, a sense of treachery, loomed through the shadows and the silence in Gethsemane. Jesus said to his disciples, "Sit here while I pray." Then taking Peter, James, and John with him, he walked further into the shadowy garden. He "began to be distressed and agitated. And said to them, 'I am deeply grieved, even to death; remain here, and keep awake.' And going a little farther, he threw himself on the ground and prayed." (See Mark 14:32-35.)

That Jesus prayed that night did not surprise his companions. Prayer was his custom; communion with God was the source from which his life and mission flowed. Repeatedly during his public ministry Jesus had withdrawn from crowds of strangers and from his friends to spend hours, sometimes whole nights, in prayer with his Father.

On that last night in Gethsemane, however, Jesus' prayer may have puzzled and frightened his friends who were accustomed to his confident, authoritative courage. That night he prayed "that, if it were possible, the hour might pass from him. And he said, 'Abba, Father, for you all things are possible; remove this cup from me; yet, not what I want, but what you want.'" (See vv. 35, 36.)

His prayer was an anguished cry from the depths of his heart as he struggled to accept and fulfill the will of his Father. The hour he pleaded might pass from him marked the moment when God would give his Son into the hands of people who could choose to receive him or reject him. Torn by his love for his Father, his commitment to gather a people for the kingdom of God, and the shameful, pain-filled death he faced, Jesus endured his agony on the rough, cold ground of Gethsemane.

His mission had ended in failure. Jesus knew he would be in the power of his most vigorous and determined opponents. They would seize him, accuse him of blasphemy and treason, and ultimately hand him over to the judicial authority of Rome whose punishment for traitors was swift, terrible, and merciless. The long-anticipated hour had come, just as Jesus repeatedly had warned his disciples: "The Son of man will be handed over to the chief priests and scribes, and they will condemn him to death; then they will hand him over to the Gentiles to be mocked and flogged and crucified" (Matt 20:18-19).

As the terrible reality was breaking before him, our Lord shrank from accepting the cup of failure his Father asked him to drink. With night and grief descending around him, Jesus cried out to God just as generations of his people had pleaded before him in their hours of desperate need, confident that the Lord listened to the prayers of the just.

> Give ear to my prayer, O God;
> > do not hide yourself from my supplication.
> Attend to me and answer me;
> > I am overcome by my trouble.
> My heart is in anguish within me,
> > the terrors of death have fallen upon me.
> Fear and trembling come upon me,
> > and horror overwhelms me.
> > > Psalm 55:1-2, 4-5

Jesus experienced his own weakness, for the Incarnate Son came among us "in the likeness of sinful flesh" (Rom 8:3). Our Lord was like us in all things but sin. It was from the depths of a very human response to rejection, failure, and impending death that he struggled. He knew fear and trembling in the darkness of Gethsemane. He felt the horror of evil as the whole burden of our sin descended upon him. He recoiled from the trial and execution he faced. He agonized over the dissolution of his life work, the scattering of the small community he had gathered for God's kingdom. Everything in him cried out against drinking the cup of humiliation, defeat, and death.

The anticipation of physical suffering apparently affected Jesus less than the shattering ruin of his mission, his failure to accomplish the work his Father asked him to do. Jesus knew his disciples would flee, abandoning him and each other along with their faith in him as bearer of the kingdom and the Messiah of God. "You will all become deserters because of me this night," he told them; "for it is written, 'I will strike the shepherd, and the sheep of the flock will be scattered'" (Matt 26:31).

What mattered to Jesus was the little flock, the community of disciples he had drawn so briefly into the heart of his own self-offering. When he returned to his disciples in the garden that last night, the comfort he sought was not so much their supporting presence as the assurance that they were still together, still with him, still a community. Even in his agony Jesus was the good shepherd watching over the flock entrusted to his care.

His concern was justified, for "he came and found them sleeping; and he said to Peter, 'Simon, are you asleep? Could you not keep awake one hour? Keep awake and pray that you may not come into the time of trial; the spirit indeed is willing, but the flesh is weak'" (Mark 14:37,38).

The command, "Keep awake and pray," held far more significance than Peter and the other disciples realized. Months earlier in the wilderness of Judea, Jesus had withstood the temptations of Satan, asserting the word of God against the wily suggestions of the evil one for the success of his mission. In Gethsemane the devil, seizing the "opportune time" (see Luke 4:13), confronted Jesus with temptation. This time the testing was directed not only against the Master but also his disciples, the community of "those who have stood by me in my trials" (22:28).

Their love for Jesus was sincere; their spirit indeed was willing. Peter proclaimed with ringing bravado to Jesus' prediction of his denials, "Even though all become deserters, I will not. Even though I must die with you, I will not deny you" (Mark 14:29, 31). But Peter's flesh, his very humanness, like that of his companions, was weak. None of the disciples understood their Master; none could sustain faith in a Messiah who must suffer to save his people.

In the Garden of Gethsemane the disciples slept while Jesus struggled to accept and embrace the will of his Father. He prayed, crying out for the help of the Father he loved as he followed the dark, lonely path marked out for him. Jesus personified the just one whose trust is in God and whose foundation is a rock of faith. He remained awake, alert in prayer to his Father's will.

Of itself prayer means opening one's entire being to the loving presence of God, becoming a dwelling place for the Lord. Prayer constitutes an offering of oneself to communion with God that his will may be fulfilled in and through the one who prays. One who prays enters into a continuing act of loving, confident faith in God, and gives everything to his service. In communion with the Lord one takes on his concerns. Love and service flow to and for others, fulfilling the kingdom precepts to love God above all else and any neighbor as oneself.

In Gethsemane Jesus, praying through his agony, still offered himself in love to the service of God. His life was for God and for others. His whole existence, his very being expressed God's love for his people. He became in his agony the completely loving, faithful response of all human beings to God. In Jesus the call of God and the total response of humankind coincided. In Jesus loving obedience, loving service even to death, would make the promised kingdom of God a reality for all the world.

The long struggle in the garden drew Jesus into the unfathomable mystery of almighty God to endure with unbounded trust all that would happen to him. From his communion with the Father the Son drew strength and courage. He remained alert, watching and praying during the time of testing. His disciples, however, slept so deeply that when the Master returned a second time, "they did not know what to say to him" (Mark 14:40).

Perhaps the sight of his closest friends united in the hour of trial only by their sleep clarified Jesus' response to the Father as he returned to pray a third time. Now he wholeheartedly embraced God's will. Only by drinking the cup, by doing as God asked, could he complete his mission. Giving himself totally into the hands of the Father, Jesus trusted that God's love would not let him go. From the emptiness of death he would become the source of life for the community he had gathered, the chalice of God's salvation of the world.

Jesus' willingness to undergo the struggle, to be put to the test and in prayer to triumph over temptation, protected his disciples from the dark powers he encountered in his passion. His prayer for his own whom he loved to the end delivered them from evil. "I am not asking you to take them out of the world, but I ask you to protect them from the evil one" (John 17:15).

Ultimately our Lord's concern as he faced the hour of his passion and death was for his disciples and through them for us who believe in him through their word. At the Last Supper Jesus gathered a community, uniting them to himself and to each other in one offering to the Father. "Holy Father," he prayed, "protect them in your name that you have given me, so that they may be one, as we are one" (17:11).

What matters is communion with God, which means communion with one another. That is why the Incarnate Word embraced and assumed the burden of our humanness, our sin and suffering, our failures and our death. In the darkness of his bitter agony in the garden our Lord descended to the depths of our humanity to lift all that we are into the forgiving, healing love of God, into his own filial communion with the Father. Jesus' prayer held his community within an embrace of infinite love, as he prepared to meet the terrible suffering that lay before him.

Within the mysterious communion of prayer God's response is always the gift of hope. Even while night descended on his life and work, Jesus, the obedient, faithful servant, could glimpse the first streaks of dawn and the morning star rising above the horizon of his Father's kingdom. No one experienced the mystery of communion in God's love for his people more deeply than the Mother of Jesus. From the beginning she proclaimed, "Let it be with me according to your word." She never questioned what her *yes* to God would mean to her own future; she simply lived each moment in fulfillment of her promise to God, in the obedience of faith.

Mary heard the word of God and kept it. She was awake and alert to possibilities, ready to choose the way of the Lord. Sorrow, pain, and fear were mingled with the joy of her life. She endured the testing and the suffering this world demands of one whose being proclaims the greatness of the Lord and whose life is given lovingly to his service.

In the midst of our often easy living, in our fear of dying, we of the twentieth century tend to place self-protection above service, self-preservation above obedience to God. We dissemble before the possibility of suffering, reluctant to surrender even a portion of our existence for fear the whole might be swallowed. Yet we know, for our Lord taught us, that life is worthwhile only when we cease to cling to it, when we are willing to give of ourselves that everyone might share in the loving communion of life that is God's gift to us.

St. Paul wrote to the Christians of Rome, "I appeal to you therefore, brothers and sisters, by the mercies of God, to present your bodies as a living sacrifice, holy and acceptable to God, which is your spiritual worship" (12:1). Christ our Lord calls each of us to live out the gift of life we have received in the obedience of faith, to become with Mary his Mother and the Apostle Paul willing servants of our Father.

God's Word spoken within us and within the community of his Church may force us to struggle with doubts and weakness. Yet as we pray, wrestling in darkness with his Word, agonizing over the choices before us, our Lord reminds us that he too prayed in anguish before he showed the depth of his love by giving his life to save us from our sin.

We are a people of prayer. We spend a lifetime repeating with Jesus from the depths of our being:

> Our Father in heaven,
>   hallowed be your name.
> Your kingdom come.
> Your will be done,
>   on earth as it is in heaven.
> Give us this day our daily bread.
> And forgive us our debts,
> As we also have forgiven our debtors.
> And do not bring us to the time of trial,
> but rescue us from the evil one.
>   Matthew 6:9-13

In communion with God we too receive the grace of hope rising like the morning star in our hearts, and strength to lift our eyes beyond the shadows of painful, merely human struggles and see the bright light of dawn heralding the coming reign of God.

In fear and trembling before the last enemy, death, but with infinite love, Jesus prayed on the last night of his life for his Church, for all of us who believe. Because he trusted and was faithful, because he obediently fulfilled his Father's will and took on himself the dark forces ranged against him, Christ's Church is founded on rock and the gates of hell shall not prevail against it. Jesus' prayer in the Garden of Gethsemane was answered; the word he had spoken was fulfilled.

> I did not lose a single one of those whom you gave me.
> John 18:9

Jesus Is Scourged

He Was Despised and Rejected
Isaiah 53:3

On the last night of his life Jesus departed from Jerusalem with his remaining followers as soon as the ritual Passover meal had ended. His action, which was contrary to the law requiring them to remain in the Holy City for the night, symbolizes Israel's rejection of its Messiah and Savior. He deliberately left the protection of Jerusalem's encircling walls, which that night sheltered the whole family of Israel.

In Jesus the Word of God came into the world, but the world did not know him. He came to his own home, but his own people did not receive him. On the night of Passover, the great gathering festival of his people, he left his home, Israel, and moved out into the chaos and darkness of the surrounding night.

"I have come as light into the world," Jesus had cried, "that everyone who believes in me should not remain in the darkness" (John 12:46). But many in Israel loved darkness rather than light, and in the persons of its religious leaders rejected the bearer of light and truth. By going out of Jerusalem on the night of Passover, Jesus became the outsider his people judged him to be. He placed himself not only with the outcasts and sinners of history but also with the very people who rejected him, the people who remained in the darkness and chaos of sin.

By lingering in Gethsemane, a place well-known to his betrayer, Jesus deliberately allowed events to control him; he set in motion the events that would overtake him. And when he rose from his prayer in the garden, he was prepared to meet the dark forces arrayed against him with confident courage.

As Jesus rejoined his sleeping disciples, all was quiet in the garden where moonlight still flickered gently through the trees. But from the slope below came the murmur of voices and the rasp of many footsteps on the rocky ground. Torches flared intermittently. Judas Iscariot was climbing the Mount of Olives with his new associates, certain he would find the friend he had betrayed in the peaceful garden.

The voices sounded louder and louder. Metal clashed on metal—Judas' men were drawing their swords. Jesus, concerned as always for his disciples, hastened to wake them. "Are you still sleeping and taking your rest?" he cried. "See, the hour is at hand, and the Son of Man is betrayed into the hands of sinners. Get up, let us be going. See, my betrayer is at hand" (Matt 26:45-46).

As he spoke, the crowd of men surged toward him through the trees, Judas at their head. Jesus stood with his sleep-befuddled disciples while the angry orange glare of torches drew nearer. Judas and his posse quickly surrounded them, seeming to loose on Jesus all the world's evil and trouble. The forces of darkness pressed closer and closer upon him until he bore the grievous weight of them all.

> My foes encircle me with deadly intent,
> Their hearts tight shut, their mouths speak proudly.
> They advance against me, and now they surround me.
> Their eyes are waiting to strike me to the ground.
>
> Psalm 17:9-11 [NAB]

Concealed behind the glare of their torches the crowd waited expectantly. "At once Judas came up to Jesus and said, 'Greetings, Rabbi!' and kissed him" (Matt 26:49). It was a signal. Judas had twisted the ageless precious expression of love, trust, and friendship to his own treacherous ends. "The one I will kiss is the man; arrest him" (v. 48).

Violence exploded around Jesus. Men rushed up to lay hold of his arms. Simon Peter drew his sword, slashed at the nearest man, and cut off his ear. Jesus would have none of it. He told his impetuous disciple to put up his sword and asked those who seized him, "Have you come out with swords and clubs as if I were a bandit? When I was with you day after day in the temple, you did not lay hands on me. But this is your hour and the power of darkness!" (Luke 22:52-53). With that the disciples edged back into the darkness and fled from the garden, leaving their Master and friend in the unyielding grip of his enemies.

Moon and stars now shone on the spectacle of the triumphant crowd hustling its prisoner down the Mount of Olives, across the Kidron Valley, and back into Jerusalem. Torches and lanterns lighted their way through the narrow streets. Behind the glare came a furtive figure. Simon Peter still followed his Master, but not too closely.

Jesus was returned to the protecting walls of Jerusalem in the midst of a hostile crowd. Unprotected and alone, he seemed helpless against defeat by the powers of darkness. The violence and stupidity of human sin that surrounded him on the mountain clung to him through the streets of the city and rushed him into the house of the high priest, Caiaphas.

There Jesus waited, a prisoner, while night wore its weary way toward dawn. He stood alone while the high priest and the council "were looking for false testimony against Jesus so that they might put him to death" (Matt 26:59). At last two witnesses came forward and, twisting words Jesus had spoken about himself, claimed, "This fellow said, 'I am able to destroy the temple of God and to build it in three days'" (v. 61).

Jesus made no answer to the charge. Then the high priest said to him, "I put you under oath before the living God, tell us if you are the Messiah, the Son of God" (v. 63).

To this demand Jesus replied, "You have said so. But I tell you, From now on you will see the Son of Man seated at the right hand of Power and coming on the clouds of heaven" (v. 64).

That was enough for the high priest. He tore his garments, crying, "He has blasphemed! Why do we still need witnesses? You have now heard his blasphemy. What is your verdict?" They answered, "He deserves death" (v. 65–66).

For some members of the council, the Sanhedrin, Jesus represented a serious threat to the Law of Moses and to the sacred tradition of Israel. The high priest commanded Jesus to deny any claims to be the Messiah. When Jesus affirmed his own truth, they heard blasphemy. This was a man who not only broke the Sabbath laws but encouraged others to do the same. He was the false prophet; he must be destroyed before he corrupted the people.

Even the rabbis who believed that Jesus came from God were bewildered by his actions, uneasy about his teachings. Nicodemus, the teacher of Israel who had visited Jesus at night, could respond only, "How can these things be?" (See John 3:1-14.)

Political concerns motivated other members of the Sanhedrin. This Galilean rabbi could be the focus of a rebellion, lead an uprising against Roman authority. Already he might be causing serious problems for the nation. Roman authorities tolerated the religion and cultures of subject peoples, but dealt ruthlessly with rebellion against the Empire. The high priest, Caiaphas, held his powerful office only at Roman pleasure. He had to be a model of cooperation in order to achieve and maintain his status.

The Sanhedrin included some collaborators, men who sought the favor of the hated Romans even at the expense of their people. The accusations against Jesus, the willingness of the chief priests and elders to seek false testimony against him, suggest a personal concern for maintaining the local balance of power.

The leaders of Israel were determined to destroy Jesus. In their minds he had said enough to condemn himself. He had blasphemed; he had abandoned the Law of Moses and his Jewish heritage. No longer was he a son of Israel; he was an outcast, the object of hatred and contempt. Since he deserved death, members of the Sanhedrin were free to abuse Jesus, to heap insults on him and treat him with contempt. They "spat in his face, and struck him; and some slapped him, saying, 'Prophesy to us, you Messiah! Who is it that struck you?'" (Matt 26:65-68).

For Jesus, mission and life were ending in the helpless humiliation of failure and degradation. The hands that healed and comforted were tightly bound. The voice that commanded demons to depart and soothed tormented hearts with calm compassion was stilled. Bruised and battered by the blows of his accusers, the One whose life revealed the merciful love of God for his people could look for no mercy from them.

> I looked for pity, but there was none;
> and for comforters, but I found none.
> Psalm 69:20

Even the one friend who had followed the crowd hustling Jesus to the house of the high priest deserted him. Peter entered the courtyard and finding a place among the servants and guards, sat warming himself by a fire, for the night was chilly. Three times he was recognized as a follower of Jesus; three times, with increasing vehemence, Peter denied he even knew the man. With his hour upon him Jesus was alone, as alone as the sorriest outcast of human history.

When morning came, all the chief priests and the elders of the people "conferred together against Jesus in order to bring about his death. They bound him, led him away, and handed him over to Pilate the governor" (Matt 27:1-2). Presenting him to the Roman as a would-be king, a rebel, and a traitor, they sought to guarantee the total destruction of Jesus and whatever following he had. If the governor condemned him to crucifixion, the man and his works would be wiped from the memory of the people. According to the Law, "A hanged man is accursed by God" (Deut 21:23).

Jesus who went about doing good, offering love and hope to every human being, stood outside the boundaries of human dignity, placed there by the blind refusal of his compatriots to see in him the Messiah for whom they waited. The walls of the Holy City no longer embraced him within the family of Israel; like the son of the vineyard owner, he was cast out to be killed. Rejected and condemned he became, "a worm and not human; [he was] scorned by others and despised by the people" (Ps 22:6). In the darkness of Gethsemane our Lord assumed the whole burden of our sins. With his condemnation by the Sanhedrin he became the victim of our sin, suffering the abuse heaped upon him by the leaders of Israel, who held him in their power.

In the brutality and violence our Lord endured from the moment of his arrest to the moment of his death on the cross the malevolent power of sin is displayed in some of its grimmest forms. Jesus received "the iniquity of us all" in order to redeem us, and the scourge of human sin battered the One who was sinless.

> But he was wounded for our transgressions,
>   crushed for our iniquities;
> upon him was the punishment that made us whole,
>   and by his bruises we are healed.
>   Isaiah 53:5

The scourging of Jesus by Roman soldiers was not just a continuation of brutal mistreatment and humiliation. The governor, Pilate, unconvinced of the prisoner's guilt, first intended to "chastise" the man, presumably for having been charged however falsely with crimes against Rome.

There was even a mocking touch of compassion in the terrible stripes Jesus received. They were eventually part of his sentence, because such a scourging weakened the condemned man or woman and hastened the cruel process of dying by crucifixion. The soldiers who scourged Jesus were competent and efficient. This was just one more task in the day's work, routine business in a very unimportant corner of the world.

For Mary his mother, for his disciples and friends, for all who love and serve the Lord, the memory of Jesus bound and dragged before his enemies, mocked and beaten, condemned and scourged, is painful and tormenting. Knowing that a beloved child, a friend, a master has been forced to suffer savage, unjust punishment leaves one in a state of horrified shock and numb sorrow.

But this man is the Son of God, the long-awaited Messiah. This most perfect of all human beings, the Holy One of God, stood judged by his accusers as less than human. It was easy for them to subject him to inhuman treatment. The violence Jesus endured appalls Christians all the more, because they experience in their own lives the mystery of his redeeming sacrifice.

This outcast, now abused and battered by his people, came among us with the fire of God's infinite love burning within his heart. His life was one continuous offering of God's mercy, of forgiveness, healing, reconciliation. He undertook his mission in order to bring estranged humankind back to God, to embrace everyone in his peace.

Jesus' proclamation of the Father's kingdom was a call to hope for anyone caught in the web of sin and the suffering that is its consequence. In his Son God's love confronted the evil that drives us apart, and overcame it. He came to free us from the entangling grip of sin, to open a way for us to begin anew within the infinitely compassionate and merciful love of our heavenly Father.

Our Lord lived what he proclaimed; he personified the kingdom of God. He came to seek and save the lost, and thus he spent his time in their company. Jesus welcomed everyone. Inevitably and wonderfully, public sinners, tax collectors, and prostitutes were among those who came to receive the healing forgiveness and the new life he offered them.

In first-century Israel, however, the righteous man who obeyed the Law and followed the traditions of his ancestors never knowingly associated with sinners for fear he would be defiled by their presence. Personal contacts were limited to the upright who respected all the details of the Law.

Thus the scribes and Pharisees expressed outrage when Jesus dined at the home of a new friend, the former tax collector Matthew. "Why does your teacher eat with tax collectors and sinners?" they demanded of his disciples. Jesus answered for himself, "Those who are well have no need of a physician, but those who are sick. Go and learn what this means, 'I desire mercy, not sacrifice.' For I have come to call not the righteous but sinners" (Matt 9:11-13).

Table fellowship expressed a covenant relationship, a union of hearts among those who shared a meal. By accepting the hospitality of Matthew and breaking bread with him and his friends, Jesus offered the forgiveness of God to the repentant sinner; he offered salvation. In the company of Jesus and his disciples Matthew no longer had to be bound by his outcast status to a life of sin. Our Lord freed him to embrace a new life, and the one-time sinner became an apostle, one of the twelve foundation stones of Jesus' Church.

Our Lord offered the merciful love of God to people as he found them. In the least of his brothers and sisters Jesus saw not the tough, disfiguring, outer layer of sin, but the human person whom God had fashioned in his own image and likeness. His eyes saw the poverty, despair, and sickness that made outcasts, ne'er-do-wells, and public sinners of God's people. He sensed in the forlorn wisps of humanity thronging about him the longing of a human heart for reconciliation and peace. The love of Jesus called forth the goodness long hidden within outcasts and sinners, and brought about their repentance and conversion.

Once, when Jesus was dining with Simon the Pharisee, a woman of the city, who was a sinner, entered the house bearing an alabaster flask of ointment. Standing behind Jesus as he reclined at table, "weeping, she began to wet his feet with her tears, and wiped them with the hair of her head, and kissed them, and anointed them with the ointment." She performed for Jesus the service his host had failed to offer.

The upright Simon was concerned that his guest was unaware he had been defiled by the touch of a sinner. But Jesus said to him, "I tell you, her sins, which were many, have been forgiven; hence she has shown great love." To the woman he said, "Your sins are forgiven. Your faith has saved you; go in peace." (See Luke 7:37-50.) How much the woman knew about forgiveness and compassion, how little the righteous Pharisee.

It was religious people, experts in the Law like the Pharisee, who failed to understand Jesus' teaching and the true meaning of his deeds. The very ones who might be expected to recognize the Messiah did not know him. Even John the Baptist wondered in his prison cell, and sent two of his disciples to ask, "Are you the one who is to come, or are we to wait for another?" (Luke 7:19). Jesus answered them, "Go and tell John what you have seen and heard" (v. 22).

Generations of God's people have heard and seen all that Jesus said and did. Everyone has experienced the joyful healing and the freedom his forgiveness and merciful love bring to the repentant sinner. We find it relatively easy to grasp the meaning of that love in abstract terms, but we experience difficulty translating our abstractions into lived Christian faith. Human weakness combines an acute sense of sin in someone else with dullness and myopia as far as one's own failures are concerned.

Sin remains a powerful force in human life. It operates subtly, twisting objective reality toward one's personal view of things; it turns intentions, words, and deeds into exercises in self-righteousness. Like the members of the Sanhedrin, who accused and condemned Jesus, many people tend to trust their subjective view of the world, to place themselves at the center and the God they claim to worship outside. Each of us is tempted to follow a selfish will rather than seeking first the will of God and his kingdom. As long as our world view remains our own, not God's, Jesus' friendship with outcasts, his readiness to forgive and to heal, may appear to us to be as reprehensible when it is manifested today as it was to religious people two thousand years ago.

The forgiveness of sins is an essential element in the good news of God's kingdom; it is central to the gospel of Christ. Jesus said, "I have come to call not the righteous but sinners to repentance" (Luke 5:32). "Naturally, this does not mean that he excludes the [righteous], but that there is no such thing. People who do not regard themselves as sinners are non-existent for salvation; or rather, for them salvation consists first of all, of admitting their sinfulness."[1]

The first call of Jesus' public ministry centered on this necessity: "The time is fulfilled, and the kingdom of God has come near; repent, and believe in the good news" (Mark 1:15). It takes humility and clarity of vision to recognize that one is a sinner just like anyone else. One who is blinded by self-righteousness is not likely to recognize the Savior, nor will that one see and hear the truth he brings.

Jesus made just this point with the parable of the tax collector and the Pharisee. The two men were praying in the Temple at the same time. Each man prayed sincerely, but it was the tax collector who recognized his sinful state and his responsibility for it. He asked for God's mercy and went down to his house justified in the sight of God. For the Pharisee, myopically convinced of his righteousness, there was simply no space for God's mercy. Full of his own goodness he did not go down to his house justified. This way of thinking tends to narrow one's view of others' faults and to restrict the mercy one is willing to offer. Which of these persons, which one of us, would extend compassion and comfort to the imprisoned, battered prophet from Galilee?

Jesus' sometimes baffling ways of reconciliation overturned the apparatus of forgiveness established by long practice not only in his time but down through the ages to our own day. He was the wholly just man who embraced all our sinning and in the power of God's love triumphed over it. Our salvation depends upon our recognizing this great act of merciful love, a love far greater than all our sinning.

God's love in Jesus reaches beyond the boundaries of human guilt to call forth tears of contrition. Such was the experience of the woman who anointed Jesus' feet with precious ointment. Such was the experience of Peter: When Jesus looked at his friend who had just denied he even knew him, the cock crowed, and Peter, overcome with remorse and grief, went out and wept bitterly.

The compassionate love of our Lord is a sign of God's reign, a new reign of justice seasoned by mercy. God the Father "has rescued us from the power of darkness and transferred us into the kingdom of his beloved Son, in whom we have redemption, the forgiveness of sins" (Col 1:13-14).

For this, Christ Jesus our Lord came among us, suffered, and died. His words and deeds revealed the compassionate, merciful God who wants to draw all people to himself, to lift them into the full light of eternal life. Through his Son, condemned, despised, and rejected, the Father still embraces us within the healing circle of his love.

Blinded by our human prejudices and faults we sometimes prefer the darkness. Like the members of the Sanhedrin we too can reject the Lord when we encounter him in unlikely forms, when he comes to us in the least of our brothers and sisters. We can remain closed to the sinner, the outsider, because we forget the compassionate, forgiving presence of God in our lives, healing and reconciling, easing the anguish of our continuing struggles with sin.

As God has forgiven us, we must forgive one another; that is central to Christian life. The mercy God has shown us must radiate in and from the community gathered in the name of his Son who died pleading forgiveness for those who rejected him, cast him out, and killed him.

Jesus of Nazareth is the Lamb of God who takes away the sins of the world. His Father hears the cry of those who know their sinful state and call upon him, "Lord, be merciful to me, a sinner." We who laid the grievous stripes of our sinning on our Lord and Redeemer find in him forgiveness, love, and the blessed peace of his Father's kingdom.

NOTE

1. Romano Guardini, *The Lord*, trans. Elinor Castendyk Briefs (Chicago: Henry Regnery Company, 1954) 129.

Jesus Is Crowned with Thorns

Behold Your King

John 19:14

The pale light of early morning brightened the skies above Jerusalem. Through the city streets came a group of high-ranking men with a bound prisoner. The chief priests and the leaders of the Sanhedrin were marching Jesus of Nazareth to the headquarters of the supreme Roman authority in Judea to deliver him for trial before the governor, Pontius Pilate. They already had judged him: The man was guilty of blasphemy because he made himself God's Son; he was a false prophet who deserved the sentence of death by crucifixion.

When the chief priests and elders actually confronted Pilate, the religious charges of blasphemy and false prophecy had twisted. The accused man proclaimed a kingdom; his compatriots presented him to Pilate as a would-be king who caused turmoil and unrest among the people, someone who might lead a rebellion against Rome.

To these leaders of Israel the idea of God reigning through a Galilean teacher was blasphemy. But to Pilate the kind of kingdom Jesus proclaimed as well as the intentions of its ruler would have presented ominous possibilities. The Roman governor almost certainly was aware that this Jesus of Nazareth was the man who had started a near-riot in the Temple by overturning the tables of the moneychangers and driving the sellers of animals from the courtyard with a whip. Jesus had acted to drive out those who had made his Father's house into a house of trade. (See John 2:16.) His motives were religious, not civil. But for that very reason he would have drawn the concerned and annoyed attention of Pilate.

Religious turmoil was a fact of life in first-century Palestine, keeping Roman governors and their military forces constantly alert for potential troublemakers. Under normal circumstances Pilate governed Judea from Caesarea Maritima; he was in Jerusalem at the time of Jesus' arrest to strengthen the Roman garrison there during the highly charged, emotional days of the Passover, which celebrated Israel's escape from slavery in Egypt to the freedom of the Promised Land.

Pilate appears in history as a particularly ruthless man, a harsh governor with no more than mediocre abilities. Luke mentions "the Galileans whose blood Pilate had mingled with their sacrifices" (13:1). His cruelty eventually attracted imperial notice, and Pilate was summoned to Rome to explain his excesses.

Whatever his authority, his fears, and his ruthless nature may have inclined Pilate to do, the Gospels make it clear that in the trial of Jesus the governor encountered ideas and forces far beyond him. Concerned for order, stability, personal status, Pilate grappled blindly and stubbornly with earthly appearances. He was well aware that he faced an antagonistic group of men determined to see the prisoner condemned to death. At best his motivation was self-protection.

When the trial before Pilate began, Jesus was the only person present who knew exactly what was happening. No one among his judges and accusers foresaw, as he did, that their actions would crown their prisoner Messiah-king and open his way into the glory of the kingdom he proclaimed with his life.

During the trial (John 18:28–19:16) the chief priests and elders remained in the courtyard of the governor's headquarters (the praetorium) in order to avoid the ritual impurity they would incur by entering a Gentile dwelling just before Passover. Jesus was taken before Pilate inside the praetorium. Pilate thus was forced to move in and out of the praetorium during the trial, going out to hear the stubborn, angry accusations of the Sanhedrin and returning inside to talk to the accused man.

Pilate was the first to call Jesus "King of the Jews." The leaders of Israel described their prisoner as "an evil-doer," a habitual criminal. To them the kingly title was blasphemy; to Pilate it was political and suspect. "King of the Jews" was a title Jesus never claimed or sought. During his trial, however, he did not deny it; rather he attempted to explain its true meaning, its higher reality.

> My kingdom is not from this world. If my kingdom were from this world, my followers would be fighting to keep me from being handed over to the Jews. But as it is, my kingdom is not from here.

Immediately Pilate seized a key word and charged, "So you are a king?" Jesus answered:

> You say that I am a king. For this I was born, and for this I came into the world, to testify to the truth. Everyone who belongs to the truth listens to my voice.

The words contained a plea, that Pilate also listen to the truth, and an offer, the saving grace of God who is Truth.

Pilate was too wary, too suspicious to listen. He fell back on contempt: "What is truth?" He could not recognize in Jesus "the way and the truth and the life," the revelation and manifestation of the dawning kingdom of the Most High God.

The governor's attitude remained political, but he realized that whatever else the prisoner might be, he was not guilty of the crimes for which he was on trial. The man simply did not fit the usual pattern of rebel leaders so dreaded by the Romans. Pilate therefore attempted to placate the waiting religious authorities and the crowd gathered in the courtyard by offering to release the King of the Jews for them. They promptly demanded the release of a notorious prisoner, a real habitual criminal and insurrectionist, Barabbas. It was at this point that Pilate, thwarted in his intentions and baffled by events, had Jesus flogged. The arbitrary cruelty was a major concession to the demands of the council leaders.

The brutal flogging left Jesus in bewildered, trembling shock. As he stood there, dazed and dull, idle Roman soldiers who had witnessed the punishment stirred themselves to make him an object of ridicule. If Pilate called this sorry figure "King of the Jews," his soldiers would crown him. With a borrowed military cloak and a crown gingerly assembled from thorn brush the men mocked Jesus with a travesty of the homage given to the Roman emperor. "They kept coming up to him, saying, 'Hail, King of the Jews!' and striking him on the face."

To Pilate the battered, ridiculous man looked more pathetic than sinister; he presented no threat to Rome or to Israel. He made another attempt to free Jesus. Going outside once more he said to the waiting crowd, "Look, I am bringing him out to you to let you know that I find no case against him."

The sun stood high in the sky, glaring down on the men assembled in the courtyard of the praetorium. Its bright rays flashed from the helmets of Pilate's soldiers and danced over the determined faces of Jerusalem's religious leaders. The crowd waited silently, their eyes drawn to the bedraggled prisoner as Roman guards led him out to stand before them under the warm spring sunlight.

He appeared dazed, still reeling from the shock of flogging and brutal treatment, with wounds still fresh on his body. He wore the purple cloak. The crown of thorns pressed rudely around his head had opened numerous scalp wounds from which rivulets of blood trickled down his bruised and dirty face. Jesus, the anointed of God, had been made a caricature of a king, a lord of misrule, a fool. Pilate's scorn hung on the tense air: "Here is the man!"

The Roman governor saw only a sorry excuse of a king, a fitting ruler for an impotent Israel firmly under the control of the Empire. Jerusalem's leaders saw a false prophet and a troublesome blasphemer who deserved no pity. Their shouts, "Crucify him! Crucify him!" resounded through the praetorium.

While Pilate struggled to remain neutral before the truth confronting him, their determination never wavered. Each sign of weakness, each concession made them more vehement in shouting down the governor's excuses for wanting to release the man he knew was innocent. "Take him yourselves and crucify him; I find no case against him," Pilate retorted.

The chief priests and elders answered him, "We have a law, and according to that law he ought to die, because he has claimed to be the Son of God."

Now more afraid than ever Pilate went back to appeal for help from the prisoner, threatening his silence with the challenge: "Do you refuse to speak to me? Do you not know that I have power to release you and power to crucify you?"

But Jesus would not compromise truth. He answered, "You would have no power over me unless it had been given you from above."

Still Pilate sought to release this troubling prisoner, while the shouts of the chief priests and their associates demonstrated their sense of growing ascendancy over the vacillating Roman governor. They cried out, "If you release this man, you are no friend of the emperor. Everyone who claims to be a king sets himself against the emperor."

The accusation was subtle but serious. Pilate indeed had presented Jesus to his accusers as a king. However scornful his intentions, his actions might well be interpreted differently in Rome, when a carefully worded report of the incident arrived there from Jerusalem. Pilate was convinced; he would give in to the demands of the accusers.

For the last time the governor returned to the courtyard prepared to sit in judgment of Jesus. As he took his seat, Pilate proclaimed with more contempt for Jewish leaders than appeal to their sense of justice:

Here is your King!

Surely he knew his words would add fuel to the determination of those who wanted Jesus crucified.

Immediately they reacted, "Away with him, away with him, crucify him!"

And the mocking voice of the governor demanded, "Shall I crucify your King?"

The chief priests answered, "We have no king but the emperor."

The contest of wills had ended. The supreme Roman authority in Judea had capitulated to the demands of the men he purported to rule. Pilate held the power, but when he compromised the truth he also compromised his capacity to judge and to rule. Of his own free will he refused to listen to the innocent Jesus. Thus he was forced to pay heed to his accusers.

The chief priests had what they wanted; the Galilean false prophet would be crucified. But the earlier words of the condemned man to Pilate now held an ominous tone: "The one who handed me over to you is guilty of a greater sin." With their insistence, "We have no king but the emperor," Israel's religious leaders renounced their covenant with God. At that moment the ritual slaughter of Passover lambs was beginning in the Temple.

Generations before Israel had proclaimed God its king. Now its leaders condemned his Son whom God sent to bring them salvation according to his promise. They condemned the Redeemer to a shameful death, greeting the long-awaited Messiah with cries of anger and hate: "Away with him! Away with him! Crucify him!" The men who refused to enter Roman headquarters for fear of defilement that would prevent them from eating the Passover that evening had set the stage for the true Passover, the sacrifice of the spotless, unblemished Lamb of God on the altar of the cross.

In the center of the courtyard the condemned man still stood, weary and suffering through the tedious morning trial, the torment and humiliation. All that remained for him was the journey to Golgotha and the slow process of dying nailed to a cross outside the gates of the city he loved.

The sun beamed down upon his thorn-crowned head, warming his torn shoulders beneath the purple cloak of mockery.

> He had no form or majesty that
>   we should look at him,
> nothing in his appearance that
>   we should desire him.
>
>   Isaiah 53:2

But for those who loved him the sunlight glaring upon the head of Jesus crowned with thorns radiated a fiery halo around the head of a king. In that rejected, abandoned failure of a prophet God still reigned.

Pilate called him king. His soldiers crowned him. Pilate himself, as he sat in the judgment seat, presented the king to his people. In the eyes of the world this king was a foolish caricature whose royal fantasies had come to naught. To the faithful, Jesus condemned to shameful execution remained the Incarnate Son of God, the heir of David's throne and the eternal, triumphant King.

Jesus' kingdom is not of this world, nor is it from the world, but it most certainly is in the world. On Good Friday only the despised, rejected, thorn-crowned Son of Man trusted the promise of God's kingdom, stretching far beyond the boundaries of the world he came to save. His kingship served a far higher, far greater authority than that of the men who conspired to condemn him.

When Christ Jesus came into our world, he emptied himself to be born in the likeness of human beings. He shared our human condition, and like any human being he grew and matured primarily through the choices he made throughout his life.

> Although Son of God in the Spirit from his human beginning, he had yet to become what he was, to consent freely to the mystery of his sonship, always accepting his identity from his Father, and receiving power from him (cf. Jn 5:36; 10:25), uttering his Father's words (cf. Jn 14:24; 17:14) and living on the daily bread of his will (cf. Jn 4:34), finally accepting, in death, no longer to exist except through the Father who begets him.[1]

The One who called God *Abba*, Father, was truly *Son*. He spoke of himself as "the Son." The title "is not the expression of any power of his own claimed by Jesus, but the expression of the total relativity of his existence."[2] Jesus came *from* God to be *for* others. His entire existence was being sent, being given, and thus he emptied himself to take the form of a slave, living totally from his Father, becoming completely his servant. Jesus lived not for himself but for us and for our salvation. Through him the love and truth of the Father flowed, unimpeded, unchecked, springing up to eternal life for the world he came to save.

The mystery of Jesus' sonship reached a climax in the hour of his passion and death, when, "he humbled himself and became obedient to the point of death, even death on a cross" (Phil 2:8). Behind the cruel, mocking coronation by unwitting Roman soldiers Christians glimpse the true dignity of the One who came to save his people: the King of kings and Lord of lords.

Christians can grasp what Pilate, the chief priests, and the elders could not see: the kingly dignity of Jesus is expressed in service. "As king he is a servant and as the servant of God he is king."[3]

Christ calls disciples to himself not to receive status or privilege, which would mock the gospel and the kingdom. Rather, we are drawn by Christ to serve the Father. If we truly serve God, we also serve one another. This, as Jesus taught his disciples, is the meaning of true greatness:

> You know that the rulers of the Gentiles lord it over them, and their great ones are tyrants over them. It will not be so among you; but whoever wishes to be great among you must be your servant, and whoever wishes to be first among you must be your slave; just as the Son of Man came not to be served but to serve, and to give his life a ransom for many.
> Matthew 20:25-28

In Jesus our God revealed himself as the love that seeks the lowest level in order to raise up what has fallen under the weight of sin, to lift the weary and heavily burdened peoples of this world toward the bright skies and boundless horizons of his kingdom. His power transforms human life; his love sets us free from slavery to sin and sets our feet on the path that leads to life. In Christ Jesus we have a King who invites us to become children of our heavenly Father, heirs with him to the glorious fullness of life. He chooses us because we are weak in order to make us strong, for his power is made perfect in weakness (2 Cor 12:9).

To Pilate this was foolishness. Power meant control, command, enslave, release or crucify; power gave him a competitive edge in the perennial struggle for status within the Empire. Confronted with truth, the Roman could only sneer, doubt, and finally compromise.

Followers of Christ know that the truth that sets them free flows in the power and wisdom of love expressed in the gift of self to the service of God and his people. Kingly dignity is loving service, and true freedom calls us to become like Christ Jesus who lived for others. For Christians to reign is to serve; it is to recognize that, "by His incarnation the Son of God has united himself in some fashion with every human being."[4]

Herein lies the meaning of human dignity, the truth of human existence. Pope John Paul II wrote, ". . . in Christ and through Christ human beings have been made more fully aware of their own dignity and high rank; aware too of the nature-transcending value of their own humanity and the meaning of their own existence."[5]

The tormented Jesus in the mock trappings of earthly power still stands for the "others" he came to save. Through the centuries he has remained the friend and champion of his rejected, humiliated followers, those whom the world regards as refuse, fools, slaves, and outcasts. The prisoner who was taunted and ridiculed in the Roman praetorium on an April morning two thousand years ago is the beggar dying on a street in Calcutta, the disturbed vagrant muttering from a park bench, the abandoned juvenile delinquent, the lonely victim of AIDS or cancer.

Our thorn-crowned Lord loves all of us without exception. He makes each of us his brothers and sisters, grants us the grace of his presence whether it radiates from us or lies hidden behind a lifetime of illness, sin, and poverty. Some of us may be, as Mother Teresa expressed it, "Christ in distressing disguise," but all of us are called to embrace with Christ each person we meet, to live as he lived, from the Father for others.

James Baldwin once said, "It is a terrible, an inexorable law, that one cannot deny the humanity of another without denying one's own." That is what happened in the Roman praetorium. Civil authority, military forces, and religious leaders made a mockery of their own religious and cultural heritage, when they scorned and derided Jesus of Nazareth, denied him human dignity, and cast him out to be executed as a slave.

The kingdom of Jesus is not of this world, nor is his kingly dignity from the world. His kingdom embraces a reality that the world, bound in pride, envy, and arrogance of petty power, can neither recognize nor receive. Jesus did present a threat to Pilate, Caiaphas, and the worldly powers they served. He called for abandonment of worldly priorities and the enslaving manipulation of minds, an end to the tyranny that exploits the human beings created by God in his image and likeness.

> Christ comes before us as one who brings to human beings a freedom based in truth, as one who delivers them from all that curtails, diminishes, and, as it were, breaks off this freedom at its roots in the soul, heart and conscience of the person.[6]

As the burning midday sun radiated fiery light from the tangled, tormenting thorns crowning the sacred head of our Savior-King, so God's light shines through the lives of those who serve him in his Son. Jesus came to bring us life to the full. Those who are his servants offer life to each of his beloved sisters and brothers without distinction, life in all the wonder, promise, and freedom of the people God created us to be and to become.

Under the reign of God, as Mary sang in her *Magnificat*, it is the hungry who are fed, but the rich go away empty. The mighty are cast down, while the lowly are raised up. Our Father's kingdom belongs to the meek, the mournful, the poor in spirit, the pure-hearted, and the peacemakers who are the salt of the earth and the light of the world. The men and women who hunger and thirst for righteousness, justice, truth, who are reviled, persecuted, and slandered for the sake of their King will find blessing in him and great reward in heaven. (See Matt 5:3 and following verses.)

In this kingdom the last are first, and the King is servant of all. He is the one whose regal glory shines from his bruised face and bleeding head, setting his thorny crown aflame with the love that will not let one of his people go.

NOTES

1. François-Xavier Durrwell, *Holy Spirit of God: An Essay in Biblical Theology*, trans. Sr. Benedict Davies, O.S.U. (London: Geoffrey Chapman, 1986) 37.
2. Ratzinger, *Introduction to Christianity*, 167.
3. Ibid., 163.
4. *The Church in the Modern World*, 22.
5. John Paul II, *The Redeemer of Man*, 11.
6. Ibid., 12.

Jesus Carries the Cross

Take Up Your Cross and Follow Me
Matthew 16:24

The condemnation of Jesus led immediately to preparations for his execution. There were no appeals, no farewells, no offers of comfort. Pilate handed the Messiah-King over to those who would crucify him, and that was the end of his concern in the matter.

Roman soldiers quickly settled the heavy crossbeam on Jesus' shoulder and pushed him into position between two prisoners already burdened as he was and waiting in the courtyard. "And carrying the cross by himself, he went out to what is called The Place of the Skull, which in Hebrew is called Golgotha" (John 19:17). The distance was not great, but Jesus, exhausted by brutal treatment and rapidly losing strength, struggled for footing on the rough paving stones of the narrow streets leading to the city gate. The Roman centurion and his detachment forced passage for their charges through the crowds of people still streaming into Jerusalem for the Passover.

Progress was tedious as the men moved through the gate, onto the dusty roadway, and then up the path leading to a rocky hill. From its summit upright beams slashed black shadows against the sunlit sky. Prisoners and escort toiled up the hill of Golgotha and stopped beside the grove of upright beams. Jesus' way of the cross had brought him from the city of his Temple to the place of the skull.

Behind him, back to the River Jordan and the dynamic moment of his anointing by the Spirit, lay the long way of the cross he had walked during the months of his public ministry. Now the mission begun in bright hope was ending in failure. All that remained was the business of dying, nailed to the crossbeam he painfully balanced on his shoulder.

Except for the indifferent Roman soldiers and the two prisoners who would die at his side, Jesus bore the cross alone. Most of his closest friends had fled in panic; one disciple had denied with an oath that he even knew his Master. The community gathered with so much care was scattered; months of preaching and teaching seemed to have borne no fruit.

The condemned man was not without some support, hesitant and timid as it was. Jesus' few remaining followers, "all his acquaintances, including the women who had followed him from Galilee, stood at a distance" (Luke 23:49) from the grove of upright beams, looking on as life was slowly, painfully taken from their Master.

The disciples had left everything, rejoicing to be caught up in the wonderful excitement and promise of the amazing man who called them to proclaim with him the coming kingdom of their God. Now, frightened and bewildered, they watched from a distance that made them indistinguishable from the crowds milling outside the city gate. Over and over in their memory Jesus spoke of his coming humiliation and passion. Over and over they heard his clear warnings and their own easy dismissals: "God forbid it, Lord! This must never happen to you" (Matt 16:22).

What the disciples so blindly ignored was happening now before them. The Master they hoped "was the one to redeem Israel" (Luke 24:21) had been delivered up by their chief priests and rulers, and condemned to death. The "prophet mighty in deed and word before God and all the people" (v. 19) staggered under the weight of the crossbeam he bore to his crucifixion.

Hopes, dreams, the life they had known as disciples of the Messiah lay in ruin. The momentous journey with Jesus of Nazareth led not to the glorious kingship they eagerly anticipated, not to honors and dignity for the loyal adherents of a victorious ruler. Their commitment brought them face-to-face with defeat and death for the friend they loved.

The contrast between Jesus and his disciples is nowhere more marked than in their responses to the coming of his hour: the Master never faltered in faithful service; his disciples were overwhelmed by fear and the instinct for self-preservation. The way of the Cross culminated a testing, a trial as it were, under which Jesus stood firm while his followers for the most part collapsed. The idea of a Messiah who could and would be crucified lay beyond their limited understanding, their little faith.

For Jesus who spoke only the word "from the Father who sent me," and whose "food is to do the will of the Father . . . and to complete his work" (John 14:24; 4:34), crucifixion completed his mission. Death came to him from the life he lived, the circumstances of his day, and his own commitment to his Father's kingdom.

Jesus' trust in God was perfect; he summoned disciples to trust in him, to make with him a journey of faith. Unlike the rabbis and teachers of his day Jesus did not simply attract a school of eager young men who would absorb his teaching and then establish their own circles of followers. He called men and women into a unique relationship with him. His "Follow me" began an enduring communion founded on trust in the Word, the Person of God's Messiah. Those whom he called experienced not an invitation to join an interesting religious movement, but a dynamic, creative, living Word urging instant response. The first disciples, Simon and Andrew, responded that way. "Follow me and I will make you fish for people," Jesus said. "And immediately they left their nets and followed him" (Mark 1:17-18).

In time the disciples undertook their own missions to proclaim the coming kingdom and heal the sick, but they did so only in the authority given them by Jesus. At no time were they or any later Christians to establish a "school" separate from the life and teaching of the Lord. Christ was himself the content and the form of their life and mission. He told them, "Those who abide in me and I in them bear much fruit, because apart from me you can do nothing" (John 15:5).

Christian life always depends on the personal relationship of the believer with God the Father in Christ Jesus his Son through the Holy Spirit. The kingdom of God draws near to us, because its prophet and teacher dwells in our midst; we know him and hear his call enabling us to be his disciples. As Jesus reminded the Twelve: "You did not choose me but I chose you" (v. 16).

Jesus defined his life in terms of his relationship with God. He came from the Father; his life and mission were for others. He kept nothing for himself. He sought no identity of his own, saying, "The Father and I are one" (10:30). "The Son can do nothing on his own, but only what he sees the Father doing; for whatever the Father does, the Son does likewise" (5:19).

Jesus called his followers to share his communion with the Father. ". . . it is the nature of Christian existence," wrote Cardinal Ratzinger, "to receive and to live life as relatedness, and thus to enter into that unity which is the ground of all reality and sustains it."[1]

Christian discipleship is predominantly a matter of the heart. In Hebrew thought *heart* referred not to the seat of emotions or the bodily organ, but to the center of one's life, the ground of one's being, the source of one's identity and personhood. Thus when the Lord calls disciples to follow him, he claims the whole person. When we respond by giving our heart to the Father in and through his Son, our entire being is caught up and welcomed into their communion. "Those who love me will keep my word," Jesus promised, "and my Father will love them, and we will come to them and make our home with them" (14:23).

Where Christ finds a dwelling place of faith in the heart of a disciple, it is the disciple who finds a home. Those who receive God's Son and believe in his Word receive the power to become children of God. (See John 1:12.) The Christian is a member of God's household. Jesus makes us his brothers and sisters who are welcomed into the place he has prepared for us in his Father's house.

Human beings, however, often fail to respond as children of God. Our sinful human condition, our continuing attempts to take hold, control others, exert power, and order creation to our own ends, deafens and blinds us. Concerned primarily for self, we can reject our dependence on God and make ourselves unavailable for discipleship.

Jesus' first disciples often demonstrated their drive for dominance, prestige, and greatness. Attempting one day to reach them, he looked over the people flocking around him and chose a child as the model for his followers. Drawing the little one to his side he said: "Truly I tell you, unless you change and become like children, you will never enter the kingdom of heaven. Whoever becomes humble like this child is the greatest in the kingdom of heaven" (Matt 18:3-4).

The humility Christian disciples are to imitate arises not so much from children's conscious awareness of littleness, as from the fact that children must live within the limitations imposed by their level of competence. Helpless at birth and dependent for several years thereafter, children have neither mental nor physical equipment to control their destiny. Their very survival depends on others. Life, growth, and development take place within a family relationship. Indeed, the quality of life for every human being is shaped to a significant extent by mother, father, sisters, and brothers.

Of necessity a child trusts the family to nourish and support life itself. Mother, father, and home stand as a child's rock of safety, the base of love and understanding launching one toward the future. Caryll Houselander wrote of childhood as the time when:

> Home and father and mother
> were God.[2]

Her words describe the loving family center to which Jesus summons his followers, asking them to put their trust in the Father and to rely upon his love and grace to guide, support, and nourish their life.

Christian discipleship is firmly rooted in reality; it demands far more than mere imitation or simple adherence to a set of behavioral standards. Jesus' disciples respond to his call from the heart, allowing his word to shape their destiny, just as a child's early life is ordered by what she or he sees and hears from parents.

No creatures are more open to the possibilities inherent in the process of growth than are children. Their wonder and delight in the world around them, their eagerness to explore and discover, reveal apparently boundless potential. Jesus urged his followers to develop a similar awareness and receptivity, and an attitude of dependence on the Word and power of God. When seventy disciples returned from their first mission proclaiming the kingdom and healing the sick, they were jubilant at their success. Jesus rejoiced because the seventy were aware of the source of their powers: "Lord, in your name even the demons submit to us!" The Father, "Lord of heaven and earth," had "hidden these things from the wise and intelligent and revealed them to infants" (Luke 10:17, 21). With a childlike, but not childish, openness Christians truly hear the Word of God and become channels for his power flowing through them to heal the sick and cast out evil spirits.

The loving trust children give to family members and friends parallels the faith in which disciples receive Jesus and his message. Both children and believers are committed beings. Mother and father are the center of their child's life; Christ is the ground of being, the center of the believer's life. Child and disciple, each finds her identity through the one in whom she has believed; each becomes who he really is on the rock of the family and the rock that is Christ.

In our harsh world with its hostility toward innocence the very characteristics that enable growth and discipleship render both children and disciples vulnerable. Love, the noblest of human attributes, and the trust it engenders indeed make us strong. But by worldly standards, love and trust often count as weaknesses and can become the sources for our most intense suffering.

No one was more aware of this than Jesus. He called those who believed in him his "little ones." To him they were important, precious beings. He insisted they were to be cherished. Their simple trust was never to be betrayed. Jesus' most vehement warning to his first disciples revealed the depth of his passionate concern:

> If any of you put a stumbling block before one of these little ones who believe in me, it would be better for you if a great millstone were hung around your neck and you were thrown into the sea.
>
> Mark 9:42

Tragically little ones sooner or later encounter the reality of the world in which they live, a world that may exact a price for their trusting vulnerability and wholehearted commitment. Jesus told his disciples: "If any want to become my followers, let them deny themselves and take up their cross and follow me" (Matt 16:24). Following the Lord means walking the way of the Cross with him; that is the cost of discipleship.

At this point the analogy of discipleship and childhood becomes difficult. We accept the realities of this world and the fact that as adults we may have to share the burden of the world's suffering; we have chosen to pay, if necessary, the cost of discipleship. Children often bear a burden imposed on them, and remarkably many of them accept the weight as willingly as Jesus himself bore all our sin.

While the world recoils from innocent suffering, it has consistently looked away from the children who bear it. From ancient times social history has recorded the ways adults use the dependence, love, and trust of children to compel them to perform disagreeable, degrading, and dangerous tasks in miserable conditions. In our own time newspapers report with numbing regularity the anguish, abuse, pain, and suffering children endure under the heavy hands of adults they love and trust.

Not all children walk a way of the Cross; not all demonstrate characteristics Jesus hoped his followers would develop. Disciples can fail to place their trust in God, neglect their responsibilities to the Lord's service. Personal goals may take first place, and Christians at various times have argued over status, betrayed the trust of little ones, succumbed to temptation, self-indulgence, and cowardice. They have denied, abandoned, and betrayed the Master they claim to serve. But the merciful love of our God embraces faltering, penitent disciples, just as the love of a family welcomes the return of an errant child.

We who believe in Christ Jesus our Lord know that our salvation comes through our Father's gift. His loving will, working through his faithful people shapes and molds us, much as the love of parents molds the life of a child. Often we struggle, not to know God's will, but childlike to do it and to accept the consequences of our faith response as they come to us from our time and place in history. It is for us to try to live the reality of our redemption in loving obedience to the Father's will. Success or failure in the worldly sense means very little for discipleship; doing the work of God is important.

Our Lord did the work his Father asked him to do, and endured disappointments, failures, and betrayal. His message scorned, his motives impugned, Jesus seemed to have labored in vain. There were times when he was hurt, even angry. He encountered and bore the burden that is the dark side of human nature in the arrogance, pride, greed, hatred, and violence that increasingly rose around him. He, the beloved Child of God, took up the Cross of human weakness and failure daily. Whatever the burdens, even the prospect of defeat and suffering, Jesus would fulfill the mission God had given him.

Christian discipleship calls for willingness to persevere, even when we discover our commitment to the Lord means pain and failure rather than peace and a sense of accomplishment. Christ has borne the grief and carried the sorrow with us, and in him the burden of our discipleship becomes light.

In our modern world with its turmoil, tension, anxiety, and stress families struggle to maintain the circle of love and protection but sometimes break apart under the strain. The child longing and needing to be cherished within a safe haven may find home a tense, uneasy environment. The family of humankind, caught in its pride, its drive to control, its power to judge and choose, may refuse a welcome to children in its midst.

An argument among his early disciples over which of them was the greatest again prompted Jesus to draw a child close to him and say, "Whoever welcomes this child in my name welcomes me, and whoever welcomes me welcomes the one who sent me; for the least among all of you is the greatest" (Luke 9:48).

This child represented not the little ones, but Jesus himself. He came among us a helpless infant, gave himself into the hands of the people he came to redeem, entrusted his life and mission to women and men who would cherish him. He asked his followers to be as open to him as they would be to their own children. Their failure to understand is poignantly apparent in Luke's story of Jesus and the children.[3]

> People were bringing even infants to him that he might touch them; and when the disciples saw it, they sternly ordered them not to do it. But Jesus called for them and said, "Let the little children come to me, and do not stop them; for it is to such as these that the kingdom of God belongs.
> Luke 18:15-16

God's love invites, compels, and enables our discipleship. Such love can overcome reluctance, self-centeredness, and fear, and open a dwelling place of faith in our hearts. Then with the loving trust of little ones we can bear all things, believe all things, hope all things, endure all things (cf. 1 Cor 13:7).

Through two thousand years disciples called by Christ have followed him along the narrow, difficult path to life. Some have struggled; some have failed. But many have lived and preached the bright vision of God's kingdom, lightened dulled hearts with the promise of salvation, replaced despair and indifference with hope and the truth that sets us free. Like children they were open, alert, and alive to the wonders God had given them.

No one bore the burden of discipleship more gracefully and lovingly than Mary, Mother of the Lord. Her response to God always manifested her obedience of faith and childlike trust in his will. She received her Redeemer as her little son, committed her life to him, followed him in early success and rejoicing and then rejection and sorrow. His way of the Cross was also hers, for her faithful love remained with him each stumbling, burdened step of his journey to death.

At times we ordinary Christians feel bound by our own limitations, bewildered like children and helpless in the face of evil, unable to effect change or even influence the people and events of our time. We are tempted to think we do very little for God's kingdom beyond bearing the Cross of our own sins and failings. Mary, the faithful disciple who proclaimed the kingdom by her life and love, teaches us that there is more to our journey than self-concern.

Love eases another's burden, when we share it by our understanding and sympathy. Forgiveness of wrongs takes away the guilt and unhappiness borne by a sister or brother. Refusal to retaliate builds peace instead of conflict. Our joy in the Lord lifts the hearts of those in sorrow.

Jesus' power, the grace of God, can work through us as it did through Mary and the saints to bear the Cross of human existence for those with whom we share our earthly journey. As one of Dickens' characters gently assured another, "No one is useless in this world, who lightens the burden of it for another."[4]

The lonely figure toiling slowly up the slope of Golgotha bore a cross weighted down with human failure, sin, disease, evil, and sorrow. Born a child of Israel, Jesus of Nazareth grew to be the faithful Israelite, the Child of God, the faithful Son whose very life was to do the will of his Father. Rejected by his own people and accursed, he became a lonely outcast no longer to be cherished within the family of Israel. But he was not entirely alone. Acquaintances and friends still kept watch from a safe distance. And from the city gate came the disciple Jesus loved, with Mary his mother, his mother's sister, Mary, the wife of Clopas, and Mary Magdalene. Beneath the cross a remnant of Jesus' scattered family gathered in love around their Lord once again.

NOTES

1. Ratzinger, *Introduction to Christianity*, 135.
2. Quoted in Ward, *That Divine Eccentric*, 324.
3. See Jerome Kodell, O.S.B., "Luke and the Children: The Beginning and End of the Great Interpolation (Luke 9:46-56; 18:9-23)," *CBQ* 49:3 (July 1987) 415–430.
4. Charles Dickens, *Our Mutual Friend*.

Jesus Dies on the Cross

Why Have You Forsaken Me?
Matthew 27:46

The daylong tread of people and beasts of burden stirred clouds of dust above the western roadway leading to Jerusalem. Dust swirled around the city gates and billowed among the people still entering the Holy City in time to keep the Passover as required by the Law. Dark clouds gathered in the sky overhead, shading the spring landscape back to the drab brown of winter.

Dust and drabness spread up and over the hill called Golgotha, where three crosses were fixed, rising black against the sullen sky. There they had crucified Jesus of Nazareth. The Messiah of God was dying, nailed to a cross with two other condemned men, one on his right and the other on his left.

Already the Roman soldiers responsible for the execution had "divided Jesus' clothes among themselves by casting lots" (Matt 27:35). Now, wrapped in their red cloaks, they "sat down there and kept watch over him" (v. 36).

Over his head a placard spelled out the charge against him, "This is Jesus, the King of the Jews" (v. 37). The mocking title provoked derisive homage, as intended. From the city wall above and from the roadway below came the jeers and taunts of those gathered to watch the spectacle. Pilgrims, merchants, and casual travelers added their insults: "You who would destroy the Temple and build it in three days, save yourself! If you are the Son of God, come down from the cross" (vv. 39–40).

The chief priests together with the scribes and elders of Jerusalem interrupted preparations for the Passover to crowd along the city wall and revile the man whose crucifixion they had accomplished: "He is the King of Israel; let him come down from the cross now, and we will believe in him. He trusts in God; let God deliver him now, if he wants to" (vv. 42, 43). Even the robbers on either side reviled him.

The taunts echoed words Jesus had heard whispering around him during his long solitude and fast in the Judean wilderness months earlier: If you are the Son of God display your power; give the people a real sign of your authority from God. With the strength he had drawn from prayer, in the desert, in the garden of Gethsemane, and in every event of his life, Jesus remained obedient, trusting in his Father's will, proclaiming the kingdom of God even as he suffered through the last lonely hours of his life. Jesus, the faithful Israelite, gave his life, abandoned his being, into the hands of God:

> In you our ancestors trusted;
> > they trusted, and you delivered them.
> To you they cried, and were saved;
> > in you they trusted, and were not disappointed.
> > > Psalm 22:4-5

Jesus' self-offering was complete; there were no boundaries to his sacrifice. He surrendered every possibility that was his, gave himself into the hostile, controlling hands of those who hated him. He mattered no more than an object to be disposed of. He was "a worm and not human; scorned by others and despised by the people" (Ps 22:6). Jesus became "the complete failure, who no longer has an inch of ground under his feet as he hangs from the cross."[1]

The Son revealed his Father's compassionate love and mercy for his people when he identified himself with the anguish and the faith of those who bore the yoke of poverty, oppression, and exploitation. His death, however, revealed the wrath of God, that abyss of separation the unrepentant sinner opens between himself and God, when he chooses his own way and separates himself from the source of life. On the cross Jesus, though sinless, willingly bore within himself the consequences of the human choice of sin. He, the Word who was with God from the beginning, separated himself from the source of his being. "As the embodiment of sin he can no longer find any support in God; he has identified himself with that which God must eternally turn away from himself."[2] He confronted the evil that drives creation into the terrifying chaos, isolation, and nothingness of death.

The cross of Jesus lifted him up alone and lonely to link heaven and earth. His arms, stretched out and out by the nails holding his wrists to the rough, wooden crossbeam, embraced an indifferent, even contemptuous world. His body, pulled downward by its own weight, descended into its dying bearing the sin, sorrow, and suffering of his people. On the cross Jesus "poured out himself to death and was numbered with the transgressors" (Isa 53:12). For our sins "he was cut off from the land of the living" (v. 8), cast out and accursed by the community of Israel.

Still and always he was Son of God coming and living only from his Father, enduring agonizing division within himself: love of God and love for a world alienated and estranged from God. Crucifixion stretched him ". . . so wide that he is simultaneously immersed in God and in the depths of the God-forsaken creature. . . ."[3]

Jesus endured his slow dying across the vast, empty,

silent space of his Father's absence. His eyes, glazing over with the approach of death, looked out upon a far darker landscape than the sullen rock of Golgotha and the grim, threatening skies above Jerusalem. The voice of his Father faded in his ears; Jesus hung from the cross engulfed in a silence far more terrible than the angry shouts of abuse and derision.

Torn between the heaven of God, the life-giving fountain, and the dry earth of humanity, he was still the Son whose life source was his Father. The dying Jesus endured infinite thirst for the God who had withdrawn from him. Father von Balthasar describes "a thirst which burns in him like eternal fire, bodily, psychically, spiritually. The Holy Spirit which accompanied him through his whole life as the Spirit of the Father is now just the enkindler of this thirst: the Spirit unites Father and Son while stretching their mutual love to the point of unbearability."[4]

That is the pain of the cross, the pain of being pulled, torn apart, rent asunder; it is the torment of a thirst no earthly drink can soothe. The one on whom the iniquity of us all was laid bore the whole terrible force of the world's sin driving him down and down through the gates of hell into the lonely nothingness of death.

Darkness covered the land about the ninth hour. Jesus cried with a loud voice, "'Eli, Eli, lama sabachthani?' that is, 'My God, my God, why have you forsaken me?'" (Matt 27:46). That last great cry from the Crucified One into the dark silence surrounding him was the cry of the Son for the Father who had left him. Alone and abandoned, burdened with our sins, God-forsaken, Jesus descended through the gates of hell, while those who mocked his tormented cry waited to see if the great prophet Elijah would come to save him before it was too late.

> And Jesus cried again with a loud voice and breathed his last.
>
> Matthew 27:50

The anguish of that God-forsaken descent into the isolation of hell echoes the cry of humankind for the God it has lost. It is our loneliness, our descent into estrangement from God, our dying, our hell, that Jesus carried in his passion and death. The cry of the dying Jesus for his Father is our cry across the abyss of our human pride, arrogance, and greed. It is the weighty sum of our manifold sins, breaking the communion of God's kingdom, destroying the peaceful harmony of the garden of his creation. Our guilt sets us apart from God, the source of our being; it separates us from each other as effectively as Jesus' enemies set him, accursed and afflicted by God, not only outside the walls of their city but outside their hearts.

As he shared our human life the Son of God also shared the waste that is our death. He experienced the apparent meaninglessness of our existence together with the pain and suffering of our sinful world. But it is our sin that weighed him down on the cross; our sin was in his dying, our separation from God dragged him down into the remote depths of hell. In the passion of Jesus God ". . . with his own divine choice accompanied the human person into the most extreme situation of his (negative) choice."[5]

In a real way the cross symbolizes the human condition. Our life is rooted in earth, but we are drawn up toward the God who made us in his image and likeness, back to the ancient garden of peace and harmony. At the same time, we embrace the life and people of earth. As human beings we are tempted to seize control, to order the world to personal advantage, and in so doing to enter upon the journey down to death.

The two criminals crucified on either side of Jesus mirror the tension, the Cross, of human existence. Luke's Gospel tells us one man railed at Jesus, "Are you not the Messiah? Save yourself and us!" The other, recognizing the justice of his sentence, knew that Jesus had done nothing wrong. To the Lord he said, "Jesus, remember me when you come into your kingdom." And Jesus said to him: "Truly I tell you, today you will be with me in Paradise" (23:39-43).

Descending to the farthest reaches of human estrangement from God, Jesus pierced the isolation and essential loneliness of sinners. In the weakness of infinite, obedient love he became one with their solitude, and broke down the barriers that kept them outside the life-giving communion of God.

Our Lord, stretched almost unbearably on the cross, reached out to the length and breadth, the height and depth, of God's creation, and gathered everything into the kingdom of his Father. No one, no thing, lies beyond the saving, healing touch of the God who eternally gives himself to and for us.

As Jesus died on the cross, the Word of God plummeted down to penetrate the silence and isolation of all who once chose their own way, refusing to hear God's Word. In that gracious, free act of dying, Jesus brought the lost from their lonely prison into communion with the Word. The Son of God lifted up the gates of death, releasing his people into the glorious freedom of being children of God. God and humankind are reconciled, made one again in the sacrificial death of Son and Brother.

The kingdom breaks into our history through the self-giving of Christ, through the sacrifice that made him an object to be disposed of. The fundamental work of Christians must be a similar self-giving, that is, death to self and life for God. The Christian gives his or her life, lays it down in faith so that God may take it to his own use.

As Christians we are part of Christ's body, the body that suffered and died for us. The baptism that draws us into the communion of Father, Son, and Spirit does so by drawing us down into the waters of death; only then can we be raised to new life.

Our path of life follows the way of Jesus, the way of the Cross. From him we learn that death to self means life for God; loss of life paradoxically becomes gain of everlasting life. St. Paul wrote to the Galatians:

> I have been crucified with Christ; and it is no longer I who live, but it is Christ who lives in me. And the life I now live in the flesh I live by faith in the Son of God who loved me and gave himself for me.
> Galatians 2:20

We come to realize that we are most truly ourselves when we lie in the earth as so many seeds dying unseen in the darkness, from which the field of wheat springs fresh and green with new life.

Experience teaches us over and over that while life in this world holds joy and beauty, it also holds sorrow. Sooner or later we will confront the dark side of our human nature, and most of us will bear a measure of suffering, grief, and pain on the journey from birth to death. It is the price we pay, because we share in the struggle against evil into which we all are born. Each of us encounters the mystery of suffering and experiences the effects of sin and evil.

If we have taken our stand with Christ and entrusted ourselves to him, we know that we may confront the evil remaining in this world in sometimes hideous and painful forms. No century has been without men, women, even children who have borne witness through their own pain to the suffering human beings are capable of inflicting on each other. Much of human anguish arises from thoughtless selfishness, rather than from malice or deliberate intention to harm.

If as Christians we live for God, then we also live for others, for the men, women, and children who may bring us happiness and contentment, sorrow and anguish, during our time on the earth. Perhaps the hardest lesson to learn is the patient suffering of the Lord we follow: "When he was abused, he did not return abuse; when he suffered, he did not threaten; but he entrusted himself to the one who judges justly" (1 Pet 2:23).

Jesus, the Suffering Servant, like the lamb of Isaiah led to slaughter, never retaliated under the abuse and torment he endured from others. We are called to a similar stance of nonretaliation no matter what the provocation may be. That is the way God asks us to reveal his truth and goodness; it is the way to the peace our Lord came to bring us.

Our century with all its advances in easing humanity's burden of pain and suffering has seen parallel developments of: increasing indifference to the desperate plight of many people who share our world; greater demand for self-advancement at the expense of someone else; the grim proliferation of drugs, weapons of death and destruction; and the development of new, more effective ways of torture. On a less dramatic but nonetheless real level, we as Christians must remember that evil is present in the world as the consequence of our choices promoting self at the expense of a neighbor. Evil touches everyone, although its effects are not always experienced equally. Each person at some time will bear suffering for another's failure as well as his or her own.

There is indeed a Cross at the heart of human existence, but our God has shared its agony. He participates in the pathos and pain of our human condition, and identifies with all those who suffer from evil of any kind. Pope John Paul II writes:

> Suffering is, in itself, an experience of evil but Christ has made suffering the firmest basis of the definitive good, namely the good of eternal salvation. By His suffering on the cross, Christ reached the very roots of evil, of sin and death. He conquered the author of evil, Satan, and his permanent rebellion against the Creator.[6]

God's gifts to humankind—faith, love, hope, knowledge, understanding, wisdom—are part of our heritage as creatures made in his image and likeness; they ennoble us. These same gifts used selfishly may be twisted into sources of anguish, and sorrow for those whom we love best in this world. Still we may cry out with and for the sisters and brothers who bear the burden of our weaknesses, and know that God will hear us.

> For he did not despise or abhor
>   the affliction of the afflicted;
> he did not hide his face from me,
>   but heard when I cried to him.
>
> Psalm 22:24

Our God never abandons us; he does not spin the universe forever outward, indifferent to its fate. He is involved in his creation, committed to the salvation of his people and their return to the peace of his garden. God hears the cry of the poor; he sees the affliction of those who suffer; and he comes down. Not only that, he goes before us so that we need not fear. In Christ he dies our death; in Christ he restores us to life. Methodist theologian Paul Schilling comments:

> Perennially, God does descend into the depths of our hells, whether we dig them ourselves or are thrust into them. But he is there with us, and in this consciousness we can find with him the way of healing.[7]

Nothing, St. Paul insisted, can separate us from the love of God in Christ Jesus our Lord. (See Rom. 8:35-39.)

Jesus' last great cry from the cross is a cry for the innocence, harmony, and wholeness humankind has lost. It is our anguished longing for communion, relationship, for the love that sustains our human existence and gives it meaning. Such love is tangible on the cross. It reaches in the bruised and broken body of Jesus across the darkness and the silence, bridging the abyss of sin and death. In the suffering body of the dying Messiah love heals our diseases and wounds. Love draws the torn fragments of our human existence into the healing oneness of community with Father, Son, and Spirit. This love, beyond all imagining or telling, changed crucifixion from an ancient symbol of terror and death into an enduring symbol of mercy and life. At the heart of the mystery of the Cross we find love, drawing all human beings to the Son of God who died upon it.

As the crucified Jesus cried out in his anguish with a loud voice, he "breathed his last," obedient to his Father to the end. "At that moment the curtain of the temple was torn in two, from top to bottom. The earth shook, and the rocks were split. The tombs also were opened" (Matt 27:50, 51-52). Darkness and chaos seized the earth again; the Word of God fell silent and departed from the world he had come to redeem. In the Temple the Holy of Holies, the dwelling place of the Most High God, was opened by the ripping of the veil that for centuries had shielded it from the sight of all but the High Priest.

Amid the turmoil it was the Gentiles, the Roman soldiers keeping watch over the crucified, who grasped the meaning of everything that had taken place. The centurion and his men "were terrified and said, 'Truly, this man was God's Son!'" (v. 54).

These words coming from the lips of men who nailed Jesus to the cross surely stirred a moment of hope in the heavy hearts of the few faithful, loving followers who stood by the cross of Jesus to be with him to the end. Their desolation was mirrored in the dark mourning of the earth around them. The heavens above were black as the disciple Jesus loved, together with Mary Magdalene and the other Mary, received the crucified body of the Lord from the soldiers, and gave it to his mother.

During the hours of Jesus' dying Mary had known the bitter thrust of sorrow piercing like the point of a sword deep into the heart of her love for her suffering son. In the stable at Bethlehem she had cradled a helpless infant in her arms. Now in the dusk and darkness around a grim rock outside Jerusalem, the Mother once more held her Child, a crucified and stiffened corpse. Again, as always, Jesus' Mother received the Word of God and kept it, obedient to his will.

Slowly the storm above Golgotha ceased, and the earth became still once again. From the city came Joseph of Arimathea, a disciple of Jesus, who had gathered enough courage to ask Pilate for the body of his crucified Master. With him was Nicodemus, the somewhat timorous defender of Jesus before the Sanhedrin, bringing enough aromatic spices for a truly kingly burial. They carried Jesus to a nearby garden, bound his body in linen cloths with spices, and laid him in a tomb hollowed in the solid rock. Then they rolled a great stone across the entrance, and departed to keep the Passover.

The disciple Jesus loved gently led his mother back into Jerusalem. Behind them the dark clouds broke, and the sky began to clear, radiating the last remaining fire of the setting sun. In the garden where Jesus slept in death the earth came to life again. From the trees bright with the green of spring birds sang gently into the twilight, and spring flowers bloomed in the tender new grass shining from the rain-washed earth.

NOTES

1. Ratzinger, *Introduction to Christianity*, 163.
2. Hans Urs von Balthasar, *The von Balthasar Reader*, ed. Medard Kehl, S.J., and Werner Loser, S.J., trans. Robert J. Daly, S.J., and Fred Lawrence (New York: Crossroad, 1982) 148-149.
3. Ratzinger, *Introduction to Christianity*, 221.
4. Balthasar, *Reader*, 149.
5. Ibid., 152-153.
6. *On Human Suffering*, VI, in *The Pope Speaks*, 29:2(1984) 131.
7. S. Paul Schilling, *God and Human Anguish* (Nashville: Abingdon Press, 1977) 257-258.

Interlude

Abide in My Love
John 15:9

In the grave they laid him, Love whom men had slain,
Thinking that never he would wake again,
Laid in the earth like grain that sleeps unseen.
Love is come again, like wheat that springeth green.[1]

At the heart of the paschal mystery stands the cross, instrument of death, tree of life. Its breadth and length and height and depth reveal the deepest mystery of human existence: God's infinite, everlasting love for humankind.

On the cross God's love is tangible, for love is life poured forth unceasingly for the other. It was not nails that held Jesus to the cross, cried St. Catherine of Siena: love held him there. The cross of Jesus stands as the ultimate expression of lifelong, self-giving love.

In the Word-made-flesh God gave to the world a lovingly obedient heart fully responsive, as God intended each human heart to be, to his gift of life. Divine love ordered Jesus' life in one enduring work of charity, *agape*, and became the channel, the living stream bearing God's redemptive love to his people. In the human heart of Jesus, powered by the breath of divine love, humankind turned to the Lord:

> I will give them a heart to know that I am the Lord;
> and they shall be my people and I shall be their God;
> for they shall return to me with their whole heart.
> Jeremiah 24:7

Jesus' last parable in the Gospel of John holds the paschal mystery within itself as a seed holds the mystery of life. He said: Unless a grain of wheat falls into the ground and dies, it remains alone, a single grain that cannot give life. But if the grain dies in the earth, it bears much fruit; new wheat, new life grows from the dead seed. (See John 12:24.)

In the paradox of this parable we realize that God's love, manifested in the life and death of his Son for the salvation of the world, accomplished far more than the simple expiation of sin. Death gives life, but the parable looks beyond this point to assert that only through death can fruit, new and more abundant life, be borne.

In the hour of his death on the cross Jesus became the seed buried in the earth, and in that same hour the power of the Spirit who accompanied him throughout his life lifted him into the Father's presence and the glory he had with him before the world began. Because Christ Jesus is raised to God, all humankind is gathered to the Father in the power of the Holy Spirit. Jesus' death gives life to the world and bears fruit in the community of believers, the people he takes with him and reconciles to God. The mystery of this fruitful death is symbolized with dramatic intensity in the events surrounding the last moment of Jesus' life, as described in the Gospel of John.

As his strength ebbed, Jesus looked around him and saw his mother and the disciple whom he loved standing near his cross. He said to his mother, "Woman, behold your son!" Then he said to his disciple, "Behold, your mother!"

From that hour, John tells us, the disciple took her into "his own" home (19:26-27). From that hour the mother of Jesus received the disciple as her son. The disciple responded to Jesus' love for him with faithful, loving obedience. Long before, at Cana in Galilee, the mother of Jesus told the servants at the wedding banquet, "Do whatever he tells you." As a result Jesus provided the first sign of his messiahship, an overwhelming abundance of rich wine (2:1-11). At the crucifixion, the seventh and last sign of messiahship, the beloved disciple and servant did as the Lord told him.[2]

Jesus' intention was not simply to secure a good home for his bereft mother. Rather the phrase, "his own," describes a people and a place where Jesus is received, believed in, and loved, a people and place distinct from "his own" who "received him not" (1:11). "His own" are found within the community of believers, the Church; they are brothers and sisters of Jesus and of the disciple whom he loved, and therefore children of his mother who in that hour became the Mother of his Church.

The gathering of this community, this family of the believers who are the fruit borne of his death, marked the end of Jesus' mission. He knew that "all was now finished." He had accomplished the work his Father had given him to do; he had revealed the Father to his people and established the community of believers who would continue to reveal God to the world, to his own. He received the vinegar offered in response to his plea, "I thirst." Then, "Jesus said, 'It is finished'; and he bowed his head and gave up his spirit." (See 19:28-30).

One of the soldiers on Golgotha pierced the side of the dead Jesus with his lance. Immediately there flowed out blood and water. The beloved disciple bears emphatic witness to the truth of this event. He saw it; he testifies to it, and his testimony is true, "so that you also may believe." (See vv. 34-35.)

For the evangelist the last breath of Jesus is the giving over of the spirit of his life and mission. It anticipates the fulfillment of Jesus' promise to send the Holy Spirit from the Father to his disciples when he has been glorified. The blood flowing from the pierced heart is the life force of Jesus and symbolizes his death, the gift of his life for his friends. From the open heart of the Savior pours the blood of a spotless, unblemished lamb, the blood of the new and everlasting covenant between God and his people, Christ's blood given for us.

The water symbolizes the Spirit, the fountain springing up to eternal life. Months earlier Jesus had proclaimed in the Temple: "Let anyone who is thirsty come to me, and let the one who believes in me drink. As the scripture has said, 'Out of the believer's heart shall flow rivers of living water'" (7:38). The evangelist comments, "Now he said this about the Spirit, which believers in him were to receive; for as yet there was no Spirit, because Jesus was not yet glorified" (7:39).

Now, in the moment of his immolation, Jesus has been glorified. The Spirit, the very love of God, flows from within Christ's body, a fountain of living water for the life of the world. *"The death of Jesus is the fullness of the Holy Spirit, now within creation."*[3] At the heart of the paschal mystery death and the Spirit of life converge. "The Spirit . . . utterly transforms death, without abolishing it, into life and power."[4]

Jesus' descent into the abyss of death consummated and epitomized the faith, love, and trust of Israel through nearly two thousand years of covenant with the living God. But the Son's love transcended the limited vision of God's people. His sacrifice answered the eternal, life-giving offer God makes to his people, and he received completely the divine Love who formed the universe, the Spirit whose breath gave life to humankind. Love transformed crucifixion from an ancient symbol of terror and death into the enduring sign of God's salvation.

Pope John Paul II has written:

> Believing in the crucified Son means 'seeing the Father,' means believing that love is present in the world and that this love is more powerful than any kind of evil in which individuals, humanity, or the world are involved.[5]

The Cross at the heart of the world is ". . . like a touch of eternal love upon the most painful wounds of man's earthly existence."[6]

In the death of his Son the God who is love enters into our world, and he remains in our midst. The Spirit of God fills the whole world just as he lives in God, as infinite love. "The mystery of the glorious cross is the mystery of the Trinity aligning itself with the world."[7]

The Spirit's love is the gathering force, incorporating those who believe into Christ, into the Trinity. The fact of God's love present among us, drawing us to him, means that we too share in Christ's salvation. That salvation means communion, fellowship, reconciliation not only with our God but also with one another. Through his Cross our Lord gives us the healing peace that draws the tattered, sordid fragments of our human existence into the new life of communion with the Father, Son, and Holy Spirit.

Jesus proclaimed a kingdom ordered and ruled by unchanging, unconditioned love. In the Spirit he remains with us always, and when we return his love, we know his presence. "Love desires no other reward than love in return; and so in return for his love God wants nothing but our love."[8] No human person, whatever his or her past, can remain a stranger or an alien to any other human person, for we share with each one and with our Lord the common ground of his passionate, unconditioned love for each of us.

> Beloved, since God loved us so much, we also ought to love one another. No one has ever seen God; if we love one another, God lives in us, and his love is perfected in us.
>
> 1 John 4:11-12

Jesus continually opened possibilities for relationship. He was a builder of community, a peacemaker whose healing love enabled the lost, the discarded, and the despised to experience the fullness of life in his Father's world. Differences in language, knowledge, place of birth, economic status, culture, and experience meant nothing to him; the good news was intended for anyone who had ears to hear it. The drive to succeed, competition, power struggles were practices alien to the work of his Father's kingdom. The Lord insisted that love of neighbor was as essential as love of self, and left just one commandment: "Love one another as I have loved you" (John 15:12). He prayed for those who would follow him that they "may become completely one" (17:23). He wanted the world to know that he loved his people and that they in turn loved him, the one who sent him, and each other.

> Everyone who believes that Jesus is the Christ has been born of God, and everyone who loves the parent loves the child.
> 1 John 5:1

Perhaps human beings in their frailty find it difficult to see the love of our God for all his children. That infinitely powerful reality lies hidden in the weakness and folly of his crucified, dead, and buried Son. Gently, inexorably that hidden love calls us to respond out of our freedom to accept or reject the redemption and new life he offers. "God's love for his children awakens love in them, so that his love itself can become a child, be born of its mother and awakened to incarnate love. The word of God calls forth man's answer by becoming an answering love which leaves the initiative to the world."[9]

We have pondered previously the need for Christians to die to self, to give their life as offering to God and neighbor. What does this mean but simply returning to God a small measure of the wondrous love he has poured into our hearts through the Holy Spirit he has given us? His is the love that is constant, pure, and passionate; his is the voice that sings to each soul as he sang to Mary, the Virgin of Nazareth, who was full of grace:

> Arise, my love, my fair one,
>   and come away.
>   Canticle 2:10

To respond to this loving call, to live by faith and trust in the Lord, is to remain with One who loves each of us as an only child. Then Christ finds his dwelling place in us; he abides in us and through us builds his community of peace, his Church. There we experience healing love, hear the good news, and receive the Spirit of love. There we can draw near to our Lord, learn of him, do whatever he tells us, and so come in his grace to the eternal life he has won for us. There the world, those others who will believe through the word of Christ's disciples, encounters the Lord and receives his salvation.

If our lives are rooted and grounded in love, then Christ is born again and again into the world through us who believe in him. The universal sign of his community is the love that gathers us together (John 13:35). The Church is the place where love is at home; it is a community of people who love. Its present reality is love gathering us, as Jesus prayed, to be one in him with the Father through the Spirit. The people drawn to Jesus as he was lifted up on his cross are forever united, inseparable from God because they are one in Christ. The love with which the Father loved his Son has been given to us, and the Son remains in us through the presence of their Spirit of love. (See John 17:26.) "Christ founded the church so that he himself could go on being present in the history of humanity precisely through the group of Christians who make up his church. The church is the flesh in which Christ makes present down the ages his own life and his personal mission."[10]

Informed by the Word borne on the Breath of God and thus animated by the Holy Spirit, the Church is forever alive, dynamic, and growing. To be found in the body of Christ is to be alive with his life and faith, his love and hope. It is to dwell within the pilgrim community of those who believe in the promise of God's reign and strive for its coming.

The Spirit's dynamic presence drives Christ's Church out to the ends of the earth and binds the present generation of believers to past generations, to the apostles and the earliest Christians, to the teaching, preaching, healing ministry of Jesus of Nazareth. In the Spirit Christ's Church speaks all languages of all times and places. Through his Church our Lord is the light of the nations. He remains the Incarnate Son present and contemporary, always founding his Church anew in the power of his Spirit, shaping it from within the hearts of the people with whom he dwells.

When we Christians share the love and the life we experience in Christ, we are sources of life and hope for others. What wonderful joy Paul must have known at the end of his long, difficult journey to Rome as a prisoner, when he realized that the people approaching him along the Via Appia were all Christians who had made the long walk from the city simply to meet him. (See Acts 28:15.) Such love is the gift Paul himself exhorted Christians to desire above all others, for it undergirds all in us that is compassionate, just, merciful, and righteous, and leads us surely into the kingdom of our God and Father.

> Love is patient; love is kind; love is not envious or boastful or arrogant or rude. It does not insist on its own way; it is not irritable or resentful; it does not rejoice in wrongdoing, but rejoices in the truth. It bears all things, believes all things, hopes all things, endures all things.
>
> 1 Corinthians 13:4-7

The cross of our Lord rises from the barren summit of Golgotha as the sign of a people, a kingdom, and a King whose rule is love and whose reign is peace, *shalom*. Under that sign we ponder the Glorious Mysteries of the rosary. The wild, extravagant, wonderful love of God has been poured into our hearts by the Holy Spirit descending among us. That Spirit of love fills the whole world and gathers all into the one fellowship that is the Church of Christ, the sacrament of communion with our God.

The Glorious Mysteries teach us that we are most truly ourselves, most truly alive, when we receive the Spirit and become the channel, the living stream of the divine Breath flowing into our world. Then heart and mind are open to the exchange that is love. Anyone who truly falls in love knows that somehow life begins anew in that moment. Before love, one simply breathed; in love, one feels wonderfully vibrant, ecstatically happy, radiant with goodness and hope. Everything about one seems new and fresh. Because we have loved, somehow we "know we have passed out of death into life" (1 John 3:14).

Love gently but relentlessly compels one to yield self to another, within a family, friendship, marriage, or consecration to God; for this love, says the Song of Songs, is strong as death. Love "binds everything together in perfect harmony" (Col 3:14). It is the firmest foundation for living, and it endures long after the tangible aspects of a life have disintegrated and scattered as dust to the four winds of the earth.

With such a gift, with our salvation assured in the passion, death, and resurrection of Christ, we who are the people of God journey with confidence into the obscurity of an unknown future. No longer are we strangers or aliens, but fellow citizens with the saints and members of the household of God, built upon the foundation of the apostles and prophets. And Christ Jesus himself is the cornerstone; in him the whole structure of the Church is joined together and grows into a holy Temple in the Lord. In him we too are being built into a dwelling place for God in the Spirit. (See Eph 2:19-22.)

Jesus is his parable; he is the grain of wheat that falls into the ground, dies, and bears abundant fruitful life. The coming of his long-anticipated hour meant death but also resurrection, the gift of his Spirit, and the gathering of a new people of God. Beneath his cross the mother of Jesus and the disciple whom he loved stand as the first fruits of a rich harvest: the women and men drawn to our Lord as he is lifted up, his own who receive him and believe in him. He himself is the peace that was his parting gift to us. In Christ we are made one; with the giving of his Spirit the love with which the Father loves the Son is in us.

> Now the green blade riseth from the buried grain,
> Wheat that in dark earth many days has lain;
> Love lives again that with the dead has been:
> Love is come again like wheat that springeth green.[11]

NOTES

1. J. M. C. Crum, in Percy Dearmer, Ralph Vaughan Williams, and Martin Shaw, *Oxford Book of Carols* (London: Oxford University Press, 1964), v. 2, 306.

2. See Joseph Grassi's restructuring of the principal sign narratives in the Gospel of John in his *Mary, Mother and Disciple: From the Scriptures to the Council of Ephesus* (Wilmington, Del.: Michael Glazier, Inc., 1988) 70-78.

3. Durrwell, *Holy Spirit of God*, 54. (Italics in original)

4. Ibid., 53.

5. *Dives in Misericordia*, 7.

6. Ibid., 8.

7. Durrwell, *Holy Spirit of God*, 53.

8. Hans Urs von Balthasar, *Love Alone*, ed. and trans. Alexander Dru (New York: Herder and Herder, 1969) 87.

9. Ibid., 117.

10. Archbishop Oscar Romero, "The Church, the Body of Christ in History," Second Pastoral Letter, August 6, 1977, in *Voice of the Voiceless: the Four Pastoral Letters and Other Sacraments*, trans. Michael J. Walsh (Maryknoll, N.Y.: Orbis Books, 1985), 70.

11. Crum, *Oxford Book of Carols*, v. 1, 306.

Resurrection of the Lord

On the Third Day He Will Rise Again
Luke 18:33

The wonder of Easter lifts us beyond the horizon of ordinary, earthly matters into the infinitely vast heart of divine mystery. Jesus of Nazareth was "crucified and killed by the hands of those outside the law. But God raised him up, having freed him from death, because it was impossible for him to be held in its power" (Acts 2:23-24). For centuries Christians have celebrated this mystery, the full revelation of God's love for us, with exultant joy, greeting the dawn of the first Sunday in the first full moon of spring with the glorious sounds of trumpet and organ, with hymns of triumphant praise and thanksgiving:

> Christ the Lord is risen!   Alleluia!
>   He is risen indeed!   Alleluia!

All Jerusalem saw this man as he "poured out his soul to death," and became "numbered with the transgressors" on Good Friday (Isa 53:12). No one saw the crucified Galilean teacher after his body was sealed in the tomb. On the third day following his death and burial, his tomb stood open; the body was gone. By nightfall that same day his disciples were certain that he was alive. The good news was as clear to them as the angel's message from the empty tomb:

> Do not be alarmed; you are looking for Jesus of Nazareth, who was crucified. He has been raised; he is not here.
> Mark 16:6

The New Testament gives no report of what took place in Jesus as he lay in the dark silence of death. As Paul VI once commented, Jesus' "new reality . . . is so far above our capacities of knowledge and even of imagination that it is necessary to make room for it in our minds through faith."[1] Early Christians were certain that the Lord Jesus lived by the power of God's infinite love lifting him from the nothingness of death to the glory of eternal life. His friends knew that God had raised Jesus from the dead, because he appeared to them as he promised: "I will not leave you orphaned; I am coming to you. You will see me" (John 14:18, 19).

Just how the resurrection came about was of little importance. What mattered was faith, believing in the good news and bearing witness to its reality.

> O the depth of the riches and wisdom and knowledge of God! For who has known the mind of the Lord, or who has been his counselor? For from him and through him and to him are all things.
> Romans 11:33, 34, 36

The story of Easter unfolds through the shadows, grief, and despair of a long night, and bursts forth in the radiant light of the morning that saw Christ rise from the dead.

The story began in the darkness when pale stars shone above the Holy City, shimmering gentle light through the trees on the Mount of Olives and over the quiet garden west of Jerusalem, where the dead slept in tombs hollowed from the rocky hillside. Earth's hard edge cast its sharp shadows against the glowing rim of dawn. The full moon seemed to hang, a faint lamp, just above the western horizon, while the cloudless sky heralded a day bright with the loveliness of spring.

Night still lingered in the city, as a woman slipped through a western gate, hurried up the road past the ominous upright beams on Golgotha, and entered the garden of the dead. Quickly, surely she moved among trees and boulders. She stopped before one of the tombs, weeping aloud as grief overcame her caution. Mary Magdalene had come to mourn the crucified Master and friend she had loved so dearly.

Above her the glow of dawn tipped the rocky outcroppings and dappled the trees with faint gold. In nearby fields the slender green shoots of new wheat glistened as the new day brightened in the west. Then the sun lifted above the horizon, sending quick shafts of warmth and light into the cold, grey shadows around the tomb.

Suddenly the weeping woman started: the tomb sealed on Friday was open. She ran from the garden to a certain house within the city. To the men who answered her frantic knocks she cried:

> "They have taken the Lord out of the tomb, and we do not know where they have laid him."
> John 20:2

Alarmed and troubled, the two men, Simon Peter and the disciple Jesus had loved, came out immediately and went with Mary to the tomb to investigate.

Both men ran, but the other disciple, running faster than Peter, reached the open tomb first. Stooping, he looked inside and saw the linen burial cloths lying there. He did not go in, but waited for Simon Peter to arrive. Peter went right in; he too saw the burial cloths, and noticed the napkin that had been on Jesus' head rolled up in a place by itself (vv. 4–7).

The scene mystified Simon Peter, and he worried: if the body of Jesus was missing, who had taken it, and why? He could foresee more trouble and danger for any friend of the false prophet and rebel Jewish and Roman authorities had just executed. But the other disciple who now joined Peter inside the tomb forgot his fears in one joy-filled moment of loving faith: he saw and believed. Then, since there was nothing either man could do, the two disciples returned to their lodgings in Jerusalem.

The grieving Mary Magdalene remained just outside the tomb. Still sobbing, she turned and saw Jesus standing in the bright morning sunlight near her, but she did not know it was he. Jesus said to her, "Woman, why are you weeping? Whom are you looking for?" (v. 15).

Grasping in her anguish for whatever help she could find, Mary assumed Jesus was the gardener and pleaded: "Sir, if you have carried him away, tell me where you have laid him, and I will take him away" (v. 15).

Jesus spoke to her, "Mary."

She knew him then: "Rabbouni," she cried, and reached out to touch him. In her gladness Mary thought the Lord had returned to take up once again the relationship his followers had always enjoyed with him.

But Jesus said to her: "Do not hold on to me, because I have not yet ascended to the Father; but go to my brothers and say to them, I am ascending to my Father and your Father, to my God and your God" (v. 17).

Mary quickly returned to the city to find the disciples. "I have seen the Lord," she said (v. 18). Then she told them the things Jesus had said to her in the garden.

Most of them doubted the story, although some surely remembered his promise, "I will not leave you orphaned; I will come to you" (14:18), and his repeated predictions, "The Son of man is to be betrayed into human hands, and they will kill him, and three days after being killed, he will rise again" (Mark 9:31).

That same day, the first day of the week, two of the disciples left Jerusalem. They already knew the tomb of Jesus was empty, but their conversation as they walked to the village of Emmaus concerned their sorrow and disappointment at his death. They did not expect to see their beloved Master again. Then Jesus himself drew near and joined them, but, "Their eyes were kept from recognizing him," even while he walked with them on the road and explained to them all the things in Scripture concerning himself. The eyes of the two disciples were not opened until evening when Jesus broke bread for them and then vanished. (See Luke 24:13-31.)

That sign was enough to send the exuberant men back to Jerusalem, wondering at their own dullness as they hurried along the dark road: "Were not our hearts burning within us while he was talking to us on the road, while he was opening the scriptures to us?" (v. 32). Bursting into the gathering of disciples and friends, they were greeted with the news: "The Lord has risen indeed, and he has appeared to Simon!" (v. 34).

Then, as they talked together of these amazing encounters, Jesus himself stood among them. "But they were startled and frightened, and supposed they saw a spirit" (v. 37). This was to be the pattern. Each appearance of Jesus was unexpected, and startled even those who already had met the Risen Lord; the disciples did not recognize him in his resurrected state.

"Jesus rose again in the same body he had taken from the Blessed Virgin, but in new conditions, vivified by a new and immortal animation, which imposes on Christ's flesh the laws and energies of the Spirit."[2]

Resurrection transformed Jesus. His friends knew him only when he revealed himself to them by a word or a gesture which called forth their faith and love. He spoke a name, as to Mary Magdalene, broke bread with his disciples at Emmaus, showed his hands and his side still marked with the signs of his crucifixion, and instructed the stubbornly doubtful Thomas to touch his wounds. Then recognition came from the heart: "It is the Lord!" Joy replaced fear, joy so amazingly full that some disciples "were disbelieving and still wondering" (v. 41). Jesus had fulfilled his promise:

> I will see you again and your hearts will rejoice, and no one will take your joy from you.
> John 16:22

Jesus let himself be seen not just by anyone but only by those whom he would entrust with a mission. Each encounter called the disciples once again to follow the Lord. Jesus "summons us to go with him. Resurrection is not an indulgence of curiosity; it is mission. Its intention is to transform the world."[3] The Risen Lord had overcome the world; now he called believers to be active witnesses to the good news of his salvation and of his kingdom. He said to his disciples: "Peace be with you. As the Father has sent me, so I send you." Then he breathed on them, and said to them, "Receive the Holy Spirit" (John 20:21-22).

The barren, empty fields of hearts deadened under the wintry weight of grief and fear suddenly burst forth in new life radiant in the spirit of Christ risen from the dead. The Lord, by appearing to his despairing disciples, gathered the broken, scattered fragments of his community into the healing embrace of his forgiving love and into the peace he brought to the world.

In that hour the disciples abandoned personal ambitions. The once reluctant, dull, and timid apostles would become fearless leaders of a dynamic new movement within Judaism. The men who fled in panic as Jesus was arrested, the friend who denied even knowing his Master, accepted the reality of the cross. Not only did they understand it was "necessary that the Messiah should suffer these things and then enter into his glory" (Luke 24:26), but they were themselves ready to bear witness to his life, death, and resurrection, even when it meant rejection, persecution, betrayal, torture, and death. Our Lord had fulfilled the prophecy of Ezekiel:

> A new heart I will give you, and a new spirit I will put within you. I will put my spirit within you.
> Ezekiel 36:26, 27

The disciples' faith in the resurrection affirms that the power of God's love is stronger than death. In faith Christians everywhere cry, "Alleluia, Christ is risen!" to a world wrapped in the shadows of death and decay. Those who believe in the good news of Easter stand confidently with the God to whom all things are possible.

We who rejoice with the dawn of Easter Sunday do not see our Risen Lord, but he encounters us in the depths of our being. Our meeting draws us to live by faith in the mystery of his resurrection, and to experience the new creation, new life, and the transformation that occurs as we dwell in ever deeper relationship with God.

Resurrection altered the flow of time and history in this world. Within the Easter mystery each believer lives, not from and for self, but from and for God whose power controls time and space, life and death. The author of First Peter exulted:

> Blessed be the God and Father of our Lord Jesus Christ! By his great mercy he has given us a new birth into a living hope through the resurrection of Jesus Christ from the dead.
> 1 Peter 1:3

In effect, Jesus remembers those who put their trust in him, when he comes into his kingdom. The Incarnate Son in the likeness of human flesh died on the cross and descended into the death to which that flesh is bound. Raised from the dead and glorified in heaven, he carried our humanity into the presence of God, and it was accepted there.

Jesus said to his disciples at the Last Supper, "Peace I leave with you; my peace I give to you" (John 14:27). "Peace be with you," was his Easter greeting to them. That peace is really wholeness, completeness, *shalom*; it is unity of being, once destroyed by sin, restored to God's creation by the death and resurrection of Jesus. In his return to the Father, the Son opened heaven once again to the creatures made in the image and likeness of God.

> The glory that you have given me I have given them, so that they may be one, as we are one, I in them and you in me, that they may become completely one.
> John 17:22-23

Resurrection is not a separate event, a reward, or a bright finish, taking place after Jesus willingly endured crucifixion and the nothingness of death. Rather, it is ". . . what is happening at the most profound level in the death of Christ . . . the profound divine dimension of the Cross, since God finally reaches man and man finally reaches God."[4]

Resurrection takes us into and reveals the deepest divine meaning of the crucifixion. Hans Urs von Balthasar wrote, "God can be dead without ceasing to be eternal life and he can, acting in this manner, prove finally that he is life and love and the goodness and grace which pours itself out in self-less self-giving."[5]

The peace Jesus gives to us is the gift of himself through the Holy Spirit, making us one again in our God. Christ is our peace:

> For in him all the fullness of God was pleased to dwell, and through him God was pleased to reconcile to himself all things, whether on earth or in heaven, by making peace through the blood of his cross.
> Colossians 1:19-20

In reality there is one Pasch of the Lord, one passage from death to life. The events that stretch from Good Friday, through Easter, Ascension, and Pentecost form one indivisible mystery. There is a paradoxical unity of Cross and resurrection: death brings fruitful life. Easter leads the Christian back to the cross, not away from it.

The Pasch, the passing over from death to life, is forever real. We enter the heart of Christian faith by sharing the death and resurrection of our Lord; we take up our cross each day in order to rise each day with him. Jesus died and was buried alone, but he was raised to life in the power of the Spirit as a community. "Rising from the dead, Jesus lived no longer merely in Himself. He became the vine of which we are the branches."[6]

Once we encounter the Risen Lord, life is no longer the same for us; our little time and history are turned around, for he draws us into his unending life, grafts us to him as the wild grapes are grafted on to the fruitful vine. Baptism, the sacrament by which we become one with Christ and receive his Spirit, immerses us in the cleansing, healing, purifying waters of death. From these waters we rise to new life, incorporated into Christ's body, the community of his Church, to share in his death and resurrection.

> Do you not know that all of us who have been baptized into Christ Jesus were baptized into his death? Therefore we have been buried with him by baptism into death, so that, just as Christ was raised from the dead by the glory of the Father, so we too might walk in newness of life.
>
> Romans 6:3-4

This was in fact the experience of Paul who wrote these lines. His conversion on the road to Damascus remains one of the great Easter stories. Christ appeared to this vehemently hostile enemy of his followers in a brilliant flash of heavenly light, and gave him insight to understand that in persecuting the disciples he also persecuted Jesus. Blinded by the light, Paul had to be led into Damascus by his companions.

His sightless state continued for three days, during which time he fasted and prayed. The once powerful persecutor waited powerless in darkness until Ananias was sent by the Lord to lay his hands on Saul and to help him regain his sight, be baptized, and receive the Holy Spirit. Baptized into Christ, Paul "clothed himself with Christ" (Gal 3:27). He himself no longer lived; Christ lived in him (2:20).

The Risen Lord brings his own life to everyone who believes in him. "He manifests his presence within us and becomes for us the source of a new life, a new identity and a new mode of action."[7] The encounter with the Risen Lord completely transformed Saul of Tarsus on his way to Damascus, "breathing threats and murder against the disciples of the Lord" (Acts 9:1). He became Paul the Apostle, "an instrument whom I have chosen to bring my name before Gentiles and kings and before the people of Israel" (Acts 9:15). His experience gave him ample grounds for proclaiming:

> So if anyone is in Christ, there is a new creation: everything old has passed away; see, everything has become new!
>
> 2 Corinthians 5:17

For Paul and for every Christian conversion and baptism mean allowing oneself to be given the form of Christ's death, to be crucified. The believer boasts and glories only "in the cross of our Lord Jesus, by which the world has been crucified to me, and I to the world" (Gal 6:14). Life becomes a continuing assent to the will of God.

If in baptism we have died with Christ in order to be united to him, then we no longer live for ourselves; we live for him. If we were buried with him, united with him in his death, then we also are "raised with him through faith in the power of God, who raised him from the dead" (Col 2:12). We stand, as Father von Balthasar expressed it, ". . . naked in death, waiting to receive the new form given to [us] as [our] baptismal robe."[8]

The central reality of the Easter mystery is love, the love driving Jesus so to dispose himself that his life became a dying, giving himself for and to others that they might dispose of him as they willed. The life of Christians who proclaim, "We are Easter people," is marked by the same disposition to be given, to submit to the driving power of the Spirit received in baptism. By their continual dying, expressed in their dedication to living and proclaiming the gospel even when faced with difficulties and dangers, the people of God manifest the life of Jesus to the world.

The Mother of Jesus stands as the exemplar of one in whom the Christ was radiantly revealed. Mary gave herself to her son's life, following where she did not fully understand, trusting when hope seemed all but lost. Abandoned, as it were, beneath the cross, and plunged suddenly into a new relationship with her son's followers, she remained the faithful witness. Her grief and suffering set her apart while Jesus lay buried in the earth.

We have no record that the Risen Lord appeared to his mother, although we would like to think he did. Perhaps, as Rosemary Haughton has suggested, Mary's flesh, which knew the incarnation of Christ in the overshadowing power of the Spirit, knew his resurrection in the transformation of the world on that Easter morning. Mary's love never demanded: enough for her to hear the witness of his friends and, without seeing, believe that her son lived, in the glory of God the Father and in the heart of her being.

By his resurrection Christ lives in each one of us. That, wrote Thomas Merton, is the "crucial importance" of the Easter mystery.

> And by living in us, He manifests Himself in the love by which we love one another. For this love is the love by which He loves us and by which He Himself is loved by the Father. The whole purpose of His mission among us is that the love of the Father for the Son be

made known in our unity and that men may see that God is love.[9]

In his resurrection our Lord draws all of us to himself in the unity and peace of his Church. He calls us to live in him and for him. His death brought life to the world. His return to the glory of the Father raises us up as branches on the fruitful vine, as new wheat to bear thirty-, sixty-, even a hundred-fold.

> Forth he came at Easter, like the risen grain,
> He that for three days in the grave had lain;
> Quick from the dead my risen Lord is seen:
> Love is come again like wheat that springeth green.[10]

NOTES

1. Pope Paul VI, April 5, 1972, quoted in Raymond Brown, S.S., *The Virginal Conception and Bodily Resurrection of Jesus* (New York: Paulist Press, 1973) n. 213, p. 125.
2. Ibid.
3. Joseph Cardinal Ratzinger, *Seek That Which Is Above*, trans. Graham Harrison (San Francisco: Ignatius Press, 1986) 65.
4. Walter Kasper, *Jesus the Christ*, trans. V. Green (New York: Paulist Press, 1977) 150.
5. Balthasar, *Reader*, 200.
6. Thomas Merton, *The New Man* (New York: Farrar, Straus & Cudahy, 1962) 168.
7. Ibid., 167.
8. Balthasar, *Love Alone*, 103.
9. Merton, *The New Man*, 194–195.
10. Crum, *Oxford Book of Carols*, v. 3, 307.

Ascension of the Lord

Declare His Glory Among the Nations
1 Chronicles 16:24

High above the earth a bird soars on outspread wings across the bright clouds of heaven, riding the wind into the dawn. It is the windhover, the superbly free creature described by Gerard Manley Hopkins in his poem, "The Windhover: To Christ our Lord."[1]

> I caught this morning morning's minion, king-
>   dom of daylight's dauphin, dapple-dawn-drawn Falcon, in
>   his riding
> Of the rolling level underneath him steady air, and striding
> High there, how he rung upon the rein of a wimpling wing
> In his ecstasy! then off, off forth on swing,
>   As a skate's heel sweeps smooth on a bow-bend: the hurl and
>   gliding
> Rebuffed the big wind.

Effortlessly gliding, swinging into the wind, hurling and bending through the air on powerful wings, the bird radiates beauty and power, grandeur and daring. The windhover heralds the dawn and claims a kingdom.

Gazing upward, the earthbound poet follows the ecstatic flight of the falcon-like bird across the heavens and is profoundly moved:

> My heart in hiding
> Stirred for a bird,—the achieve of, the mastery of the thing!

His whole being exults. In the ascending and descending flight of the windhover he sees an image of Christ, his life, passion, and glorification.

> Brute beauty and valour and act, oh, air, pride, plume, here
>   Buckle! AND the fire that breaks from thee then, a billion
> Times told lovelier, more dangerous, O my chevalier!

Memory and vision summon the poet. The call is "lovelier, more dangerous," because it is so compelling that it cannot be denied by even the most timid of Christians.

The poet realizes great acts of valor and daring are not the only responses to Christ's call. Quiet deeds born of patient, steadfast courage also radiate the glory of God's love.

> No wonder of it: shéer plód makes plough down sillion
>   Shine, and blue-bleak embers, ah my dear,
>   Fall, gall themselves, and gash gold-vermilion.

A farmer slowly plodding behind his plough turns furrow after furrow ("sillion") of dark, moist earth to shine in the spring sun. Dead embers, Christ crucified, of a once-blazing fire fall and break open to reveal the radiance of the living flame within. And just as the drab plumage of the windhover flashes "gold-vermilion" when touched by the fire of the rising sun, so Christians can light the world with the glory that comes to them from the Lord of the universe, the preacher, teacher, and healer who came to cast the fire of God's kingdom on the earth.

Hopkins' vision of the windhover in flight evokes a dynamic image of a profound mystery: the glorification of Christ the Lord. "The Windhover" mirrors the triumphant exaltation of the crucified Messiah throned in heaven at the right hand of God. The responding exultation of the poet reflects the glory of the Risen Lord present in his disciples and revealed through them. The Church celebrates this mystery as the Ascension of the Lord.

According to the Acts of the Apostles, Jesus appeared to his disciples for a period of forty days following his resurrection. During that sacred time he showed them in many ways that he was alive. He spoke to them and taught them about the kingdom of God. They were to remain in Jerusalem, he told them, to await the fulfillment of the Father's promise.

His disciples still anticipated political and material rewards. "Lord," they asked, "is this the time when you will restore the kingdom to Israel?" (Acts 1:6). But Jesus replied that such knowledge was not for them. "But you will receive power when the Holy Spirit has come upon you; and you will be my witnesses in Jerusalem, in all Judea and Samaria, and to the ends of the earth" (1:8).

When he had said this, Jesus was lifted up. As the disciples looked on, a cloud concealed him and took him out of their sight. Still they gazed upward, straining their eyes toward heaven for a glimpse of their beloved Master. Then:

> suddenly two men in white robes stood by them. They said, "Men of Galilee, why do you stand looking up toward heaven? This Jesus, who has been taken up from you into heaven, will come in the same way as you saw him go into heaven."
>
> Acts 1:9-11

The disciples returned to Jerusalem with great joy. They remained in the city, gathering together daily in the upper room where they had shared the Passover meal with Jesus, and going often to the Temple to praise God. Their interest in the coming of a worldly kingdom no longer existed.

The story of Christ's ascension seems almost fantastic to skeptics who may doubt the possibility that a cloud carried the Lord into the heavens. For the believer the cloud signifies the presence of God. The departure of Jesus in the cloud marks the climax of his hour, the culmination of his journey from death to resurrection and exaltation.

Luke's stories in the Gospel and in Acts dramatize the moment of Jesus' return to the glory he had with the Father from the beginning. The evangelist's attention is on the glorified Lord and his relation to the company of believers so joyfully coming together each day in the upper room. Indeed, the story of the ascension ponders the deepest mystery of Christ's Church.

One might begin by considering the meanings of *glory*, *glorify*, and *glorification*, words that recur in Scripture and the liturgy. Defining these words is no simple task, for they represent ancient human attempts to express something about the God of Abraham, Isaac, and Jacob, the God of Jesus Christ.

In the Hebrew Scriptures glory describes splendor of the highest degree. Glory is God's manifestation of himself in mighty acts. His infinite splendor and majestic power, the plenitude of his being, the abundance of his richness overflowing into creation all reveal his glory. We experience that glory because we live surrounded by it: the beauty and the power of nature, the splendor and mystery of the universe, the wonder of life.

God manifested his glory in the many remarkable works he accomplished in, through, and for his people. God's holiness, his goodness and greatness, his passionate concern and love for his people all express his glory. God's glory is also his presence. That presence in the cloud by day and the pillar of fire by night guided Israel through the wilderness to the Promised Land. When Solomon dedicated the Temple in Jerusalem, the divine presence came down in a cloud and rested above the ark of the covenant in the Holy of Holies.

In brief, the glory of God is God as he reveals himself to us. And he reveals himself supremely and perfectly in his only begotten Son, Jesus of Nazareth. "And the Word became flesh and lived among us, and we have seen his glory, the glory as of a father's only son, full of grace and truth" (John 1:14).

Jesus manifested the glory of God through his mighty works. The wonderful miracles by which he changed water into wine, healed the sick, multiplied loaves to feed the hungry, restored sight to the blind, and raised the dead to life were signs of God's presence. Only God can perform such amazing deeds. Only God can give life.

Everything Jesus said and did revealed the glory of God dynamically present in human history. He countered opponents who intended to stone him for blasphemy: "Even though you do not believe me, believe the works, so that you may know and understand that the Father is in me and I am in the Father" (10:38). Because God was with him, his words were spirit and life, and his deeds gave people healing, forgiveness, life itself. He glorified God by keeping the Father's word, by accomplishing the work given him by the Father, by revealing who God is.

Jesus first existed in glory and in the form of God. He did not cling to that glory but emptied himself to be born a human being. On the last night of his life he prayed, "Father, the hour has come; glorify your Son so that the Son may glorify you" (17:1). In death Jesus emptied himself, giving over his Spirit. He was completely given, totally open and thus could be filled with the Spirit of life and love. In one mighty act of power God glorified his Son, drawing him back to his side, making it clear to all who believe that Jesus is Christ and Lord to the glory of God the Father. The Cross thus glorified the Father and became the way of the Son's glorification. When you have lifted up the Son of man, Jesus said, you will know who I am. (See John 8:28.)

As the Incarnate Word, the Son of God, Jesus embodied the glory of God. While he dwelt among us, that glory became visible as Isaiah prophesied:

> And the glory of the Lord shall be revealed,
> and all people shall see it together,
> for the mouth of the Lord has spoken.
>
> Isaiah 40:5

We have seen that glory in the life of our Lord. We have seen it radiantly revealed in the still form of the sinless, crucified Christ. In a strange way Jerusalem, by lifting the Son of man on the cross, became the herald of good tidings and said to the despised *anawim* who remained with him to the end, "Behold, your God!" The placard fixed to the cross above Jesus' head proclaimed his crime in Hebrew, Greek, Latin for all nations, all people, of the ancient Mediterranean world, to understand: "Jesus of Nazareth, King of the Jews." A Roman centurion, his executioner, beholding the Lord as he died, saw the glory and proclaimed, "Truly this man was God's Son!" (Mark 15:39).

God's mighty act raising Jesus to glory affirmed his Son's life and work. In that moment our human being was transformed by the re-creative power of God's love. This transformation is living reality, not just an idea or attitude or orientation. "God's Son did not discard his humanity, but took it with him into the eternal glory. . . ."[2] In Christ human nature was lifted into the presence of God. ". . . God is not only 'supreme Being,' but supremely divine *and* human being; we must realize that man is not only human, but that the tip of his essence reaches into the unknown, and receives its fulfillment in his Resurrection."[3]

Glorified as Lord and Christ, enthroned at his Father's right hand, the position of power, Jesus could send the promised Counselor, the Holy Spirit, from the Father to be with his community. The ascension and the sending of the Holy Spirit placed the disciples and the community in a new situation and placed their relationship with Jesus, now both Lord and Christ, in a different context.

> The glory that you have given me I have given them, so that they may be one, as we are one, I in them and you in me, that they may become completely one, so that the world may know that you have sent me and have loved them even as you have loved me.
> John 17:22-23

The Lord our God is one God, the Father of glory who unites everything to himself in Christ his Son through their Holy Spirit. The glory Jesus gave to his disciples is the divine presence, the indwelling of the Holy Spirit who will remain with them forever. It is the glory of communion, "that the love with which you have loved me may be in them and I in them" (17:26). Jesus' prayer was for the community gathered as he was lifted on the cross, for his Church, and for the unity of believers in every generation. The principle of that essential unity is the glory given by God to Jesus and communicated by him to his disciples. "The Church is a mysterious extension in time of the Trinity, not only preparing us for the life of unity but bringing about even now our participation in it."[4]

The Church comes from God, exists entirely for his service, and relates wholly to Christ. Apart from its Lord the Church has no existence, just as branches have no existence apart from the vine that supports and nourishes their growth. The Church remains in Christ by the power of the Holy Spirit, and stands in the world as the place where everyone may encounter the living God. It challenges the world as Jesus once challenged his friend Martha, "Did I not tell you that if you believed, you would see the glory of God?" (John 11:40).

The community of believers glorifies the Lord, because through the Spirit the Church is the continuation of Christ as revealer of God. By its very nature the Church incarnates the life and love of the Father and the Son in the Spirit. The people of God proclaim the word and work of Christ Jesus "as burning torches proclaim the light."[5] The ascension thus can be understood not only as the glorification of the Lord but also as his commission to his disciples and through them to his Church down through the ages: Go out to all the world and tell the good news.

The Father had sent Jesus into the world to proclaim the coming of his kingdom; now the Lord Jesus sent his disciples to fulfill the same mission.

> All authority in heaven and on earth has been given to me. Go therefore and make disciples of all nations, baptizing them in the name of the Father and of the Son and of the Holy Spirit, and teaching them to obey everything that I have commanded you. And remember, I am with you always, to the end of the age.
> Matthew 28:18-20

In the context of the Church and its mission John's image of the vine and the branches takes on new and deeper significance. Glorifying God means bearing fruit, communicating life. The mission of the Church then means communicating life to others. One who remains in Christ as a branch of the vine remains in the life our Lord shares with everyone who believes. That life is never settled or complacent. To believers faith is a compellingly active and dynamic gift; it wells up as it were from the depths of their being and permeates every aspect of life as spring rains permeate the soil of the earth.

Jesus taught his disciples, "You are the salt of the earth." "You are the light of the world." He called them to be the "city built on a hill" that cannot be hidden. He did not light the lamp of faith to hide under a bushel basket; it was to remain on the lampstand giving light to everyone in the house. "Let your light shine before others, so that they may see your good works and give glory to your Father in heaven." (Matt 5:13-16.)

The salt that flavors earthly life, the light shining before the world in the Church is Christ Jesus himself, God-with-us to the close of the age. This reality is central in the mission of the Church. The words of the Voice on the mountain where Jesus was transfigured before three of his disciples, apply in every generation: This is my beloved Son; listen to him. It is to Christ and his salvation that the Church bears witness. It is his word that the Church proclaims. It is toward Christ that the Church aspires, and in Christ the Church must be found.

Jesus is the Christ anointed by God; he is the Word of God, Truth itself. On the eve of his departure he promised to send the Spirit of truth to be with his disciples forever. He "will teach you everything, and remind you of all that I have said to you" (John 14:26). Because he is Spirit of truth, he speaks, not on his own authority, but, "whatever he hears" (16:13). "He will glorify me, because he will take what is mine and declare it to you. All that the Father has is mine" (vv. 14–15).

The Holy Spirit whom Christians receive in baptism sanctifies believers in the truth. His presence empowers the Church to speak with authority of what it has seen and heard from the Father in Christ Jesus. Believers in every age owe the immensely rich heritage of Christian doctrine and tradition to the faithful witness and authoritative teaching of the first disciples, the apostles to whom our Lord entrusted the good news of salvation and on whom he breathed the Holy Spirit. The company of believers, guided by the Spirit of truth, has remained devoted to the teaching of the apostles. That Spirit-inspired fidelity of the Church through the turmoil and struggle of human history guarantees the truth of its witness in every generation.

The fidelity of the Church and its people to the mission entrusted to them by Christ is abundantly attested in the life and work of countless believers through the centuries. The letters of Paul testify eloquently to the writer's firm conviction of his call and commission from the Lord. To the Christians in Corinth Paul wrote: "But it is God who establishes us with you in Christ and has anointed us, by putting his seal on us and giving us his Spirit in our hearts as a first installment" (2 Cor 1:21-22). He insisted that he and his companions did not proclaim themselves. Rather, "we proclaim Jesus Christ as Lord and ourselves as your slaves for Jesus' sake" (4:5). We are not "peddlers of God's word like so many; but in Christ we speak as persons of sincerity, as persons sent from God and standing in his presence" (2:17).

These ambassadors for Christ speak, "not with plausible words of wisdom, but with a demonstration of the Spirit and of power, so that your faith might rest not on human wisdom but on the power of God" (1 Cor 2:4-5). What Paul and his companions imparted was "God's wisdom, secret and hidden," "things God has revealed to us through the Spirit; for the Spirit searches everything, even the depths of God" (2:7, 10). The Spirit helped them "understand the gifts bestowed on us by God," and thanks to him, "we have the mind of Christ" (vv. 12, 16).

As earthen vessels, clay jars, holding this treasure Paul and all who faithfully proclaim the gospel of God's kingdom make the life of Jesus visible in their bodies. (See 2 Cor 4:7, 11.) Faith calls all of us to bear witness to Christ's word of truth, to grow and bear fruit, communicating life to others, letting his light shine in our hearts to "give the light of the knowledge of the glory of God in the face of Jesus Christ" (4:6). By sharing the fullness of life that is his gift to us, we manifest his glory.

> We declare to you what we have seen and heard so that you also may have fellowship with us.
> 1 John 1:3

If we indeed hold this treasure, the gift of the Spirit in the teaching of Christ, we strive to conform our life to his. "Be imitators of me, as I am of Christ," Paul urged (1 Cor 11:1). Our growth as disciples is measured not by how much we know about Jesus but by the revelation of his presence through our responses to the events of daily life. There is a wisdom in sincere Christian living that reveals the meaning of Jesus for our time and place, that glorifies the Lord.

Jesus himself glorified God by his way of life; he was the fully righteous human being, the faithful Servant of God, who lived in conformity with the will of God. God's glory shines in his Son in the unfathomable richness of his magnificent love, love so powerful that it lifted the Crucified One from the grasp of death to eternal life in heaven.

The overflowing plenitude of our God is poured out for the salvation, the life, of his people. God is love; and the glory of God is that love which gives life by giving itself so completely that it can be disposed of by and for another. His will for us is simply, "Love one another as I have loved you."

> God is love, and those who abide in love abide in God, and God abides in them. Love has been perfected among us in this: that we may have boldness on the day of judgment, because as he is, so are we in this world.
> 1 John 4:16-17

When the Church is as he is, the way of the Church is: "Each individual human being, since each is included in the mystery of redemption, and since, in this mystery, Christ has united himself to each for all time to come."[6] The Church sets no limits on its love, following Jesus who told his disciples: "Love your enemies, do good to those who hate you, bless those who curse you, pray for those who abuse you" (Luke 6:27-28).

Faith manifested in word and deed actively extends Christ's love in the world. Human arguments may falter, but God, by his power at work in and through us "is able to accomplish abundantly far more than all we can ask or imagine" (Eph 3:20).

The glory of God is the enduring love that lifts despairing hearts to hope, and proclaims that each person can be sister or brother to Jesus Christ, that each is God's image, each breathes with the breath of God; each is God's work of art. Dominican Father Paul Scanlon writes of his experience with parishioners caught in an unending cycle of economic poverty: "In hearing the gospel the poor have discovered the richness of God's love and the value of their own lives. That wisdom ennobles them as well as enables them. It enables them to be free in spirit no matter how burdened in body. It is bearable because the poor carpenter from Nazareth chose to be their blood-brother."[7]

God's glory shines in the teaching and works of the apostles, in the wisdom of Paul and his companions, in the writings of the Church Fathers, in the great deeds of saints, in the lived faith of Christians in every age. Quiet, unremarked goodness, unnoticed deeds, the hidden witness of a life faithful to the teaching of our Lord also fulfill the mission of the Church and glorify God. Like the windhover, the people of God reflect the glory of the Light for all to see.

The Mother of Jesus proclaimed the greatness of the Lord from the hidden heart of her being; her spirit rejoiced in the God who is our Savior. Her response to God's call glorified him, for her life quietly reflected the advice she gave the servants at Cana: Do whatever he tells you. (See John 2:5.) Beneath the cross Jesus' mother embraced the disciples of her son, his brothers and sisters, as her children. She is thus Mother of the Church, a great ray of light revealing the life we all receive from God and the hope guiding our journey to him.

Mary prays for us as Paul prayed for his friends in Thessalonica, "asking that our God will make you worthy of his call and will fulfill by his power every good resolve and work of faith, so that the name of our Lord Jesus may be glorified in you, and you in him, according to the grace of our God and the Lord Jesus Christ" (2 Thess 1:11-12).

When he has prepared a place for us in his Father's house, our Lord will return for us just as he left us, on the clouds of heaven, bearing his divine presence to enfold us in him forever. In the meantime, we who are his Church bear the privilege and responsibility of proclaiming his good news faithfully, living in the truth of his word, glorifying the Lord our God as we journey in this world.

The exalted Jesus has given us the glory of God's love, transforming, liberating, raising us up. Our Lord takes us with him in his glorious ascent along the highway he has opened between heaven and earth, between time and eternity: a highway for our God who, like the falcon ascending the heavens in its flight, also descends again and again into the hearts of his beloved people.

NOTES

1. Hopkins, "The Windhover," *Poems of Gerard Manley Hopkins*, 69. The windhover is a kestrel hawk, a falcon-like bird of prey. Gardner and MacKenzie (267) interpret the windhover as a "symbol or analogue of Christ, Son of God, supreme Chevalier. May the human equivalents of this bird's heroic graces and perfectly disciplined *physical* activity be combined and brought to much higher *spiritual* activity in my own being, just as these attributes were once and for all transmuted in Christ." (Italics in original)

2. Romano Guardini, *The Lord*, 412.

3. Ibid., 413.

4. Henri de Lubac, *The Church: Paradox and Mystery*, trans. James R. Dunne (Staten Island, N.Y.: Alba House, 1969) 24.

5. Hans Urs von Balthasar, *The Heart of the World*, trans. Erasmo S. Leiva (San Francisco: Ignatius Press, 1979) 34.

6. John Paul II, *Redemptor hominis*, 13.

7. Paul Scanlon, O.P., *Spirituality Today*, 34:2 (Summer 1982) 127.

The Coming of the Holy Spirit

My Peace I Give to You
John 14:27

Jesus' disciples returned joyfully to Jerusalem, after his ascension to heaven. They remained in the Holy City as he had directed, quietly gathering in the upper room, praying together, and worshipping in the Temple.

On the tenth day following the ascension, the fiftieth day after Passover, Israel celebrated the Feast of Weeks, or Pentecost. Devout Jews came in pilgrimage to Jerusalem to give thanks to God for the spring harvest by offering the first fruits of their fields in the Temple. As the people of God they also celebrated the anniversary of their covenant with him and the giving of the Law to Moses on Mt. Sinai.

On the very day of Pentecost the apostles, the women, the brothers of the Lord, and Mary his mother were praying together behind the closed doors of the upper room. "And suddenly from heaven there came a sound like the rush of a violent wind, and it filled the entire house where they were sitting. Divided tongues, as of fire, appeared among them, and a tongue rested on each of them. All of them were filled with the Holy Spirit and began to speak in other languages, as the Spirit gave them ability" (Acts 2:2-4).

The rush of wind and fire and voice flared beyond the house, gathering a multitude of people, devout Jews from every nation under heaven. Amazed and perplexed they crowded around the ecstatic Galileans, for each one of them could hear the disciples telling the mighty works of God in the native language of each. As wind and fire died away, everyone, even those who sneered at the disciples' ecstatic speech as the babbling of drunkards, heard Peter's proclamation: "Jesus of Nazareth, a man attested to you by God with deeds of power, wonders, and signs that God did through him among you, as you yourselves know—this man . . . you crucified and killed by the hands of those outside the law. This Jesus God raised up, and of that all of us are witnesses. Being therefore exalted at the right hand of God, and having received from the Father the promise of the Holy Spirit, he has poured out this that you both see and hear" (vv. 23, 32-33).

His astonished listeners "were cut to the heart." Eagerly, anxiously they asked Peter and the disciples, "Brothers, what should we do?" Peter said to them, "Repent, and be baptized every one of you in the name of Jesus Christ so that your sins may be forgiven; and you will receive the gift of the Holy Spirit" (vv. 37, 38).

This gift, the mysterious force of the Holy Spirit, flows like a river of living water from the heart of Christ's love, bearing with it our forgiveness, our communion, and our peace. The Spirit is the Counselor, the Advocate, whom Jesus promised to send to his disciples from his Father. The Spirit is power from the risen and glorified Lord, the omnipotence of love poured into our hearts, healing and renewing them, transforming them with new life. The descending Holy Spirit reveals creation set free from the bonds of sin, a world in balance, restored to wholeness, integrity, and peace, *shalom*, as the words we pray in the sequence for Pentecost suggest.

The Holy Spirit descended into our human history as wind and fire, but to us he brings sweet refreshment for our earthly pilgrimage. He is rest in the midst of our toil, coolness in the burning heat of day. Like dew on the grass as evening falls, the Spirit moistens the dryness of our lives. In his presence the hardened heart softens and melts; the cold, indifferent heart becomes warm with new tenderness.

If we are stubborn, the Spirit's bending power can make us supple and flexible again. As human beings we are still inclined to sin; but should we be tempted to stray, the Spirit guides us in the path of righteousness and love. If we are sick or disabled by our own failures, the Holy Spirit heals our wounds and renews our strength; he penetrates our hearts bearing the gifts of God's healing love, restoring us to wholeness, to *shalom*.

The soul's most welcome guest remains within us, the silent, hidden, eternal love of Christ. His presence makes us eloquent witnesses of Christ's salvation, temples through whose windows and doors his grace shines to light and warm our world.

The Holy Spirit is the mysterious Third Person of the Trinity; he is not revealed as the Father is, through the Son. We do not see him, but we experience him, the one who is the eternal love of the Father and the Son. Through him we are drawn into the communion of the eternal triune love of God. The world does not know the Holy Spirit, but Jesus told his disciples, "You know him, because he abides with you, and he will be in you" (John 14:17).

By appearing to them on the evening of Easter the Risen Lord forgave the disciples who had deserted him. "Receive the Holy Spirit," he said (20:22). His word, borne on the Breath of his mouth, healed the wounds that separated them from him. He reconciled them to himself, making them one with him. Once again they were his community.

The healing of the disciples meant healing for the world languishing under the wounds of sin. With his gift of the Spirit the risen and glorified Lord also granted authority to his chosen disciples, the power of forgiveness, healing, and reconciliation: "If you forgive the sins of any, they are forgiven" (20:23).

The world's healing took place at that point in history when Jesus poured out his life to death on the cross and was raised up in the power of the Holy Spirit. As Isaiah foresaw:

> Upon him was the punishment that made us whole,
> and by his bruises we are healed.
> Isaiah 53:5

Then on Easter the Holy Spirit came to the disciples, bearing the God of love into our human history. Through them and through every believer who receives the Spirit at baptism he remains with us, extending the saving power of the Lord in every age and in every place. With the Spirit's coming the disciples of Christ could begin "to gather into one the dispersed children of God" (John 11:52).

The harvest of the Spirit, the gathering of a worldwide community, began on Pentecost. The fresh wind of the Spirit's coming opened the doors of the upper room and sent the disciples out into the world to proclaim the gospel of salvation. Peter's inspired word opened the hearts of the devout Jews in his audience, and they repented their failure to believe in Jesus. In faith they received the gift of the Spirit who drew them into Christ.

The men and women baptized on Pentecost were incorporated by the Spirit in Christ, together with the apostles, the women, Mary the Mother of Jesus, and his brothers. The healing and reconciliation Christ brought to his closest followers, through them, now healed and reconciled some three thousand people who were added that day to the company of believers.

According to the Acts of the Apostles, these earliest converts formed a vital community reflecting their oneness in Christ. They devoted themselves not only to the apostles' teaching, but to fellowship. They persevered in living a life worthy of the gospel of Christ, the gospel of love for God and one another. The believers "were together and had all things in common." They cared for one another. Those who were in want found their needs filled by those who had plenty. (See Acts 2:42,44-45.)

We may well imagine that within this fellowship a forgiving, healing spirit perdured, that its members worked and struggled to maintain their unity. The community revealed itself to the world around as the people of God, a renewed Israel, an integrated, balanced fellowship inspired and sustained in Christ Jesus by the Holy Spirit.

Significantly, the first public proclamation of the gospel after Pentecost by apostles from this company of believers followed the healing of a man lame from birth. Peter and John were going up to the Temple at the hour of prayer. They arrived at the Beautiful Gate just as the man was being placed where he could beg alms from people as they entered the Temple. When the man asked Peter and John for alms: "Peter looked intently at him, as did John, and said, 'Look at us.' And he fixed his attention on them, expecting to receive something from them. But Peter said, 'I have no silver or gold, but what I have I give you; in the name of Jesus Christ of Nazareth, stand up and walk.' And he took him by the right hand and raised him up; and immediately his feet and ankles were made strong. Jumping up, he stood and began to walk, and he entered the temple with them, walking and leaping and praising God" (Acts 3:4-8).

All the people in the Temple saw the man walking and praising God. When they recognized him, they were filled with wonder and amazement at what had happened to him, and ran to him where he stood clinging to Peter and John. Even in our century of medical marvels this wonderful healing astounds and amazes, but for the people who were there it signified a far more profound event.

The ancient world associated medical treatment and health care with religious practices.[1] Israel, in rejecting the gods of surrounding nations such as Egypt, also rejected as pagan their medical practices and systems of health care. While the Hebrew Scriptures affirm the sacredness of human life and glory in all its activities, they are indifferent to medical aid for the sick and to the value of disabled people in community life.

For ancient Israel, any deviation from physical or mental integrity made the person unclean, unable to enter the Temple and participate in the worship of the community. The sick and the disabled had fallen from a state of wellbeing into a situation that prevented them from enjoying meaningful human life. Disability and illness were regarded as punishments for sin. The disabled usually were dependent on other people for survival; some, lepers for example, were considered to be as good as dead.

Treatment in Israel was rudimentary at best: knowledge was limited; contact with the sick or the dead rendered the care giver unclean. Afflicted human beings were isolated and lonely, outsiders in every sense of the word. They had little hope that their situation could be reversed or even improved, unless God himself intervened directly. Only God can heal; only he can restore limbs that have never been whole.

The lame man expected to get something from Peter and John. His expectation was fulfilled, but instead of gold or silver he received health and wholeness, well-being, *shalom*. The healing revealed the power of God present with the apostles of the Risen Lord to heal the world, to gather its people, reconcile them to God and one another in the communion of Christ. The lame man had languished outside the fellowship of Israel, dependent, helpless, unable to share in the activities of human life. Now the outsider enjoyed the fullness of that life; he was restored to the image and likeness of God. One who had been as good as dead was born anew into the human community. With the eyes of faith he could see and one day enter the kingdom of God.

The experience of such healing is a gift not only of God's compassion but of his mercy and forgiveness. A world disordered, diseased, and disabled by sin lies behind most of the suffering endured by innocent and guilty alike. Only God can forgive sin. Jesus healed the paralysed man whose friends lowered him into the house through the hole they made in the roof, "so that you may know that the Son of man has authority on earth to forgive sins" (Mark 2:3-12). And the Risen Lord gave that same authority to his disciples with his gift of the Spirit on Easter.

As Jesus had reached out to draw outcasts and sinners into the kingdom of his Father, so his disciples would offer the same fullness of life, healing the sick, seeking the lost, proclaiming the good news to the poor, gathering the scattered flock into the one sheepfold. The lame man at the Beautiful Gate represents "the poor," the outsiders of every nation under heaven. Through Peter and John God stretched forth his hand to heal him and restore his life, just as he restores and heals our life today.

The authority to forgive sins is central to the mission of Christ's Church. Jesus told his apostles they would evangelize the world by preaching repentance and forgiveness of sins to all nations in his name (Luke 24:47). Healing is simply a sign that Christ remains with his Church, forgiving sin by opening the heart of the sinner to the presence of his Spirit. The Lamb of God takes away our sins by incorporating us into himself, by converting us to union with God. The Holy Spirit makes us one in Christ, and Christ sends his Spirit to unite us in faith to God.

To experience such healing and forgiveness is to be touched by the love that embraces not just an individual but the community. "At the point where the light of God touches a human being healing begins, not only for the individual, but through him for the whole world."[2] The healing of the man at the Beautiful Gate touched everyone who witnessed his newfound strength and joy, for he embodied a sign of the kingdom of God breaking into human history.

The healing of the lame man was the work of God, not of human beings, and a gift of faith. Peter made this clear when he seized the opportunity to proclaim the gospel. "The faith that is through Jesus has given him this perfect health in the presence of all of you" (Acts 3:16). He urged the crowd, "Repent therefore, and turn to God so that your sins may be wiped out, so that times of refreshing may come from the presence of the Lord" (v. 19). Peter and John were arrested by the annoyed chief priests and the Temple police, "But many of those who heard the word believed; and they numbered about five thousand" (4:4).

The Church of Christ is the community of women and men called together by God through the Spirit and united in the Lord. The love of God poured into our hearts unites us in Christ to God and to one another. The new reality, our communion in the eternal triune love of God, is manifested through the Church, because the Church is the mysterious yet visible sign of that communion.

The Spirit cannot unite us, cannot reconcile us to God and one another without our cooperation. The Spirit is gift and grace, holiness and peace. But he must be received, and the gifts must be lived. We live his gifts and reveal his presence within us by our love for God and one another. The compassion of God often becomes real for people when they experience a tangible atmosphere of healing and forgiveness within a community. The letters of Paul to the communities he founded still alert and urge Christians to live justly, righteously, in loving harmony with one another in order to build up the community, the body of Christ.

> May the God of steadfastness and encouragement grant you to live in harmony with one another, in ac-

> cordance with Christ Jesus, so that together you may with one voice glorify the God and Father of our Lord Jesus Christ. Welcome one another, therefore, just as Christ has welcomed you, for the glory of God.
>
> Romans 15:5-7

During our earthly pilgrimage we are a fellowship of forgiven sinners who do not outgrow their need for repentance and healing. We reveal Christ's presence in the Spirit by the love that transcends differences and divisions and expresses itself in our readiness to be channels of healing grace. "Be kind to one another, tenderhearted, forgiving one another as God in Christ has forgiven you" (Eph 4:32). The Church preaches and lives what it has received: the grace of faith, repentance, healing, and forgiveness of sins.

Christians cannot forget that they form the community of Jesus whose cross reveals that God's power is infinite love. The Church is not the kingdom in its fullness; rather it is a budding of the kingdom, a sign of its reality. Through the actions of the Church, inspired by the Spirit, Christ who embodied the kingdom is present in our world. Jesus, himself full of the Holy Spirit, "surrendered to the Father's love and it went through him as compassionate healing power."[3] The omnipotence of the Church is love giving itself away, healing and gathering the scattered children of God.

Love is the language of the Christian, the way in which one's communion with God is expressed, the way the Holy Spirit tells of his presence among us. "The Spirit is love; he is expressed in the faithful through the love he enkindles in them."[4] The Spirit is the law of God written in human hearts; through the Spirit God's love becomes the new principle of human existence, the source of our growth in Christ.

> Speaking the truth in love, we must grow up in every way into him who is the head, into Christ, from whom the whole body, joined and knit together by every ligament with which it is equipped, as each part is work-

ing properly, promotes the body's growth in building itself up in love.

Ephesians 4:15-16

The Church is the place where love is at home, but no one of its members is the whole Christ. We can neither contain nor reveal the infinite love and truth of God's Son our Savior. But we can reveal his presence as he asks and as the Spirit inspires us. Within Christ's community we are free to choose the goodness God offers us; we are free to receive his healing forgiveness, to reject temptation and the evil our society accepts. We can respond to the gifts he offers us, receive and use them for the glory of God.

Over everything we put on the love that is the Spirit's great gift to those who believe and receive him. It is love that maintains the integrity and well-being of God's people. Love encourages a spirit of harmony and balance. Loving one another we bear one another's burdens. We find grace and strength to: "lead a life worthy of the calling to which you have been called, with all humility and gentleness, with patience, bearing with one another in love, making every effort to maintain the unity of the Spirit in the bond of peace" (Eph 4:1-3).

The Holy Spirit bears the love of God into the hearts and lives of believers in every generation. In the Spirit we are born again in baptism; in the Spirit we grow and mature; in the Spirit we become the people of God who are preparing to enter his kingdom. The healing activities of the Holy Spirit suggest not the dynamic wind and fire of his coming but something far deeper and more enduring for humankind: the tender, comforting love a child seeks and finds in its mother's arms:

> As a mother comforts her child,
> so will I comfort you.
>
> Isaiah 66:13

In every culture the image of mother and child together evokes memory and trust, hope and love. This great symbol also stands for healing and peace, for *shalom*. We look on the Church, the body of Christ growing toward the fullness of life in the Holy Spirit, as Mother. And we look to Mary Mother of God as our model for Christian life. She is our Mother too, for by the gift of the dying Jesus she is the Mother of the Church.

The rich wonder of this mystery of Emmanuel, of God-with-us in the Church founded by his Son and gathered through the centuries by their Holy Spirit, seems beyond our comprehension. It is a marvel we cannot grasp even with the gifts of knowledge, understanding, and wisdom God has poured upon us. The picture of mother and child together opens the mystery and makes it just a little clearer to the eyes of the heart.

In one well-known image of Mother and Child, the icon of the Virgin of Vladimir, Mary holds the Christ close to her with one arm. He embraces her neck with both of his arms. Her face is inclined toward him; their cheeks touch lovingly. With their mouths so close together, the Christ-child breathes the Holy Spirit into his Mother. Mary does not look at her son, nor does she look at us. Her eyes see God.[5] But with her left hand she who is our Mother invites us to receive the Spirit, the Breath of life, and to enter with her into the peace of Christ, the eternal communion of divine love.

NOTES

1. I am indebted to articles in the January 1989 *The Bible Today* (27:1) for information on medical treatment in Israel and the status of the sick and disabled in the time of Jesus and the early Church.

2. Caryll Houselander, *Lift Up Your Hearts* (New York: Arena Lettres, 1978) 82.

3. Maria Boulding, *The Coming of God* (Collegeville: The Liturgical Press, 1982) 72.

4. Durrwell, *Holy Spirit of God*, 163.

5. See the profoundly beautiful reflection on the icon of the Virgin of Vladimir as an invitation to belong to God in Henri J. M. Nouwen, *Behold the Beauty of the Lord: Praying with Icons* (Notre Dame: Ave Maria Press, 1987) 31–42.

Assumption of Mary

We Are God's Handiwork
Ephesians 2:10

The sunshine splendor of the golden season spreads across the land, as the earth's slow turning draws the cycle of life and growth to its climax. Apricots and peaches ripen in the hazy humidity of high summer. Swelling grains of corn and wheat splash the green fields with their own sunlight. Black-eyed Susans, gloriosa daisies, sunflowers, and goldenrod sway their warm and brilliant beauty as the summer breezes sweep gently through garden, meadow, and prairie. The life we saw springing green and tender from the cold earth of spring grows steadily, surely toward maturity in the warm light of the sun.

With the coming of August the earth seems to slow down, to pause, gathering in the full radiance of summer to ripen its fruits. The land gradually yields its heat to the atmosphere in the wake of the retreating sun. Living creatures absorb the lingering light of summer, preparing for the darker season of death and rest. The end of the growing season lies just ahead, and the time of the harvest is near.

At the peak of this rich, warm golden season, on the edge of the earth's slow descent into the death of winter's rest, stands Mary of Nazareth, the Mother of the Lord. Her whole being filled with the Holy Spirit, Mary lived, prayed, and worked among her son's disciples. The years of concern for her little boy, the moments of bewilderment, anguish, and sorrow, had passed. Jesus' followers continued his mission, preaching the gospel of his kingdom, drawing believers into his community, proclaiming the good news to the ends of the earth.

Mary's life quietly drew to its close; yet for her the approaching end would be the beginning. Firmly rooted in earth, she was always total openness to heaven, always growing, always the handmaid of the Lord. She received the Word of God and buried it like precious seed to be nourished within the rich soil of her being and brought forth by God as new life in the fullness of time. The tree of her faith, hope, and love, blooming with the delicate loveliness of spring, had grown to maturity, and Christ Jesus himself gathered into eternal glory "the most perfect fruit and work of his redemption."[1]

On the fifteenth of August, the Church celebrates the Assumption, when Mary is taken up to heaven, and the angels of God shout for joy. In that moment the promise of the Lord was fulfilled in one human being, in his mother. Mary is one with the risen, glorified Christ in the fullness of her being.

As a mystery of faith the Assumption takes form in the realm of heart and spirit where the Spirit's gifts of knowledge, understanding, and wisdom draw one beyond the limited powers of human analysis into the flow of salvation history. It is Christian tradition, a living reality, a teaching handed down and developed within the Church from one generation to another. Tradition draws life from the presence of the Holy Spirit who teaches everything and guides the people of God into all the truth. (See John 14:26; 16:13.)

The belief that Mary was assumed body and soul into heavenly glory at the end of her earthly life grew within the Church during more than fifteen centuries. The Assumption, celebrated by Christians as early as the sixth century, is the oldest feast in Mary's honor. But it was not until our own century that the Vicar of Christ, Pius XII, solemnly defined the Assumption of Mary as revealed truth.

What we believe as Christians is the revelation of God in Christ Jesus his Son as reported by the apostolic witnesses chosen by the Lord, guided and inspired by the Holy Spirit.

> We declare to you the eternal life that was with the Father and was revealed to us—we declare to you what we have seen and heard so that you also may have fellowship with us; and truly our fellowship is with the Father and with his Son Jesus Christ.
> 1 John 1:2-3

Christ himself is both the mediator and the fullness of all revelation; in him the "deepest truth about God and the salvation of humankind shines out for our sake."[2] Through divine revelation God shares with us treasures that "totally transcend the understanding of the human mind."[3] The treasure of divine revelation entrusted by God to his Church is never static, fixed for all time. Revelation is one dynamic totality, God's Word to humankind in Christ Jesus, the Word whose infinite riches are unfolded by the Holy Spirit to the Church in every age. Tradition thus forms part of the one divine and apostolic revelation of the Lord. It grows within the Church, within the body of Christ's followers who devote themselves to "the apostles' teaching and fellowship, to the breaking of bread and the prayers" (Acts 2:42).

By his solemn proclamation of Mary's Assumption into heaven Pope Pius XII gave Christians certainty that what the Church, led by the Holy Spirit, had believed and taught for centuries indeed belongs to its heritage of divine and apostolic revelation.

The Assumption leads the believer to ponder far more than the one moment of time when Mary's earthly life drew to its close. It draws one into the mystery of our redemption, of the Church, and of our life in faith. In Mary we see the image and model of the whole, for her Assumption, which began with her death, is in fact the fulfillment of her life.

Jesus proclaimed, "I came that they may have life and have it abundantly" (John 10:10). The dogma of the Assumption assures us that Mary, the human person beloved of God and called by him to be the Mother of his Son, by his grace entered body and soul into the fullness of life with him for all eternity. She who was overshadowed by the Spirit and became the earthly dwelling place of the Incarnate Word is forever at home with the Lord of infinite glory.

Christ's work of redemption is manifested in a human person, in one of us. It was in our humanity, our flesh and blood, that our Lord was raised from the dead and taken up into the glory of the Father. The eternal glory that became reality in the flesh of Christ Jesus through him transformed the body of his mother to be like his glorious body. What God accomplished in his crucified Son by the power of the Holy Spirit he also accomplished in the Son's Mother.

Mary is "something else" and "something more" than an ordinary member of Christ's body, of his Church, because she is intimately associated with the origin, the very root, of our redemption.[4] Life came to Mary as it comes to every human being, as a gift of God. Each life traces a brief journey within the whole time of salvation history, but God sees the totality of his creation, embracing each beginning and end, each journey in his infinite vision.

In the first moment of her existence Mary received the fullness of grace, God's gift of his divine life, so deeply and completely that, when God's messenger came to her some years later, her whole being assented to the Spirit overshadowing her, and she conceived the Incarnate Word within her body and her soul. She is the Virgin Mother of the Redeemer by the grace of God and her own graced response. Mary lived that grace and made it visible by proclaiming its presence in all that she was, all that she did. God filled her life journey; her heart was open, giving room for everything. Her assent proclaimed, behold the handmaid of the Lord forever, and thus her ending was full of grace, holy, and blessed. "All that the faith says about the realization of redemption, about salvation and grace and the fullness of grace, is realized in Mary. This human person whom we call Mary is as it were the very point in the whole history of our redemption at which the saving grace of the living God descends from him into this history, and from which it is diffused over the whole of mankind."[5]

Mary's graced response to God, her willingness to become the Mother of his Son, decisively influenced the history of salvation in which we live. Her words to the angel, "Let it be to me according to your word," arise from her own free choice. God who made each human being in the image and likeness of his freedom never forces a decision, never compels obedience. His gifts allow Mary and each of us to respond freely from the heart of our being, to accept or reject the divine life he offers.

By her own free act of faith Mary received for the world the grace of the incarnation; she conceived the Son of God and gave him earthly existence. Her life from that moment became a pilgrimage of faith. Her response to God made her the earthly place of God's presence, the Temple of the Most High, the one in whose heart Christ the Savior finds a dwelling place.

Yet for all her closeness to Jesus, her daily contact with the Incarnate Son, the mystery remained. Mary could enter into that mystery only as God chose to reveal it to her, one of his little ones; she could approach the truth of her son as we must approach it, in faith.

By her act of faith Mary entrusted herself completely to God: Let it be with me according to your word. She entered into communion with God, surrendering herself to the truth of God, opening and freeing her very being to be taken over by God. Pope John Paul II wrote:

> To believe means to abandon oneself to the truth of the word of the living God, knowing and humbly recognizing "how unsearchable are his judgements and how inscrutable his ways" (Rom 11:33). Mary, who by the eternal will of the Most High stands, one may say, at the very center of those "inscrutable ways" and "unsearchable judgments" of God, conforms herself to them in the dim light of faith, accepting fully and with a ready heart everything that is decreed in the divine plan.[6]

"Faith in the obscurity of God's inscrutable ways becomes conformity with him."[7] Mary entered into communion with God, living in unity with his will as manifested in her obedience of faith. In her trusting surrender of mind and heart to God, Mary also accepted her responsibility to do God's will.

The Mother of our Lord did not always understand; the full meaning of the splendid words spoken to her by the angel at the annunciation was not apparent to her, even though she treasured the striking events of her son's young life, pondering them in her heart. Hers was a faith like that of Abraham whom Paul calls "our father in faith." Like the great patriarch through whom all the tribes of earth were to be blessed, Mary had to trust in God, hoping against hope, even as she walked in darkness. The road she traveled on her journey of faith remained obscure before her. She did not always understand, but she had heard the word of God, and she kept it.

Jesus once told his opponents, "Very truly, I tell you, anyone who hears my word and believes him who sent me has eternal life, and does not come under judgment, but has passed from death to life" (John 5:24). The faith that gives life comes from God; it convinces us of things we cannot see, as our Lord's words to his doubting disciple Thomas indicate: "Blessed are those who have not seen and yet have come to believe" (20:29).

Mary is present in the mystery of Christ because she believed. Her faith is a source of her blessedness, as her kinswoman Elizabeth so quickly perceived, "Blessed is she who believed that there would be a fulfillment of what was spoken to her by the Lord" (Luke 1:45). She never anticipated all that this fulfillment might mean. She never defined for herself the meaning of the words in which the angel described the child: He shall be great, called Son of the Most High, receive the throne of David, reign over the house of Jacob forever; and there shall be no end of his kingdom. (See Luke 1:32-33.) She simply abandoned herself, even when she stood beneath the cross, to the meaning God would give them in his own time.

"Faith is the surrender of the entire person: because Mary from the start surrendered everything, her memory was the unsullied tablet on which the Father, through the Spirit, could write his entire Word."[8] These words of Father von Balthasar describe beautifully "the immeasurable riches of God's grace in kindness toward us in Christ Jesus" (Eph 2:7), manifested in the life of Mary. They show us the loving faith of the young woman who in her quiet, simple life fulfilled her son's counsel to his followers: Live in me as I live in you.

We live in Christ by faith; we live knowing God, knowing his truth, because he has offered and we have received the gift of faith that convinces us of things we cannot see. We may not know just how we received faith; we may remain unable to explain adequately just how we came to believe; but we know we are living in faith. Faith transcends the natural intellect as a light infused by God for knowing the truth that surpasses the possibilities and demands of pure reason. Pope John Paul II said, ". . . human reason is not negated or degraded by the act of faith, but achieves its greatest intellectual heights in the humility with which it acknowledges and accepts God's infinite greatness."[9]

How simply and beautifully expressive of faith is Mary's *Magnificat* in this light:

> My soul magnifies the Lord,
> and my spirit rejoices in God my Savior,
> for he has looked with favor on the lowliness
> of his servant.
>
> Luke 1:46-48

In humility of faith Mary received the divine life, the gift of God in person. She knew she was the mother of the child who would become the Redeemer of all only by the grace of God. The young woman who rejoiced so happily with Elizabeth foresaw that "henceforth all generations will call me blessed"; but such veneration would come to her only because "the Mighty One has done great things for me" (vv. 48-49).

She is supremely the Woman of Faith, the model of the believer, because in the end it is grace, and grace alone, that matters to our salvation. Paul reminded the Church at Ephesus, and reminds Christians to this day:

> For by grace you have been saved through faith, and this is not your own doing; it is the gift of God—not the result of works, so that no one may boast. For we are what he has made us, created in Christ Jesus for good works, which God prepared beforehand to be our way of life.
>
> Ephesians 2:8-10

If anyone wants to boast, Paul told the Corinthians, let him boast of the Lord. (See 2 Cor 10:17). We do not work out our own salvation under our own power; the divine life that draws us into the sphere of the eternal God comes to us as his grace, his gift of himself. We are in effect unprofitable servants who must receive everything from God.

But if we truly receive God into our being, into hearts that at last know the Lord, then his infinite, glorious, loving presence overflows our human limits to touch and transform the lives of others. This is the essence of Christian community. Here again Mary is our model, for in receiving the fullness of God, she gave flesh to the Word and birth to the Savior of the world.

In Mary of Nazareth God and human history converge. She is God's work of art, the finest work of the redemption won for us by her divine son. All that our Christian faith says about redemption and salvation, about grace and the fullness of grace is realized in Mary. She is the image of the Church, the perfect Christian; she is the expression of what redemption means. Her graced ending was the outcome of her life on earth, her eternity won freely, responsibly, faithfully from her graced beginning.

Everything that matters is grace, and Mary is full of grace. In this she is "something else" and "something more" than the rest of us. But Mary is also and always one of us; she is the sign of what we can become by the grace of God. We too have our beginning in the love of the faithful God. Divine grace is offered to us, for God calls us to become who we are by receiving his gift of himself, his steadfast love, his kindness, mercy, and truth.

Our God gives us to ourselves. We are free in his grace to work out all that we are and may become, free to choose our life path, to make the journey, to dream and dare the impossible, to strive and achieve or fail, to know moments of struggle and ease, sorrow and joy, courage and fear. We are free to come to know him as he is. In Christ Jesus our Lord we have "access to God in boldness and confidence through faith in him" (Eph 3:12). And we pray for each other as Mary prays for us:

> that Christ may dwell in your hearts through faith, as you are being rooted and grounded in love. I pray that you may have the power to comprehend, with

all the saints, what is the breadth and length and height and depth, and to know the love of Christ that surpasses knowledge, so that you may be filled with all the fullness of God.

Ephesians 3:17-19

In the mystery of the Assumption is the promise of heaven, eternal life for those who believe, the final and enduring grace, the fullness of our God. Mary, our Lady, reveals the accomplishment of grace in the love of God for a human being. Full of grace, she is the sinless Mother of God, *Theotokos*, God-bearer. Something more and something else, her life teaches us that in the eyes of God we are more than just sinners, more even than unprofitable servants. God gives his love and grace to us as he gave them to Mary. He calls us to live in faithful expectation and loving awareness, open to every possibility. Our ending, like hers, is to be with the Lord and Savior who in his mercy leads us to his kingdom to be with him where he is, to see his glory.

The warm, golden aura hovering over the ripening earth in August reminds us that the great sign of our salvation is the Woman clothed with the sun. The Mother of God, the perfect fruit of Christ's redemption, stands as the Church in glory. She is the image of those who believe and bear fruit in eternal life, who are redeemed by the passion and resurrection of her son. In praising Mary we praise the infinite and merciful love of our God who does great things for us, his people. Holy is his name.

NOTES

1. Karl Rahner, S.J., *Mary Mother of the Lord: Theological Meditations* (New York: Herder and Herder, 1964) 83.
2. *Dogmatic Constitution on Divine Revelation*, 2.
3. Ibid., 6.
4. Yves Congar, O.P., *Faith and the Spiritual Life*, trans. A. Manson and L. C. Sheppard (New York: Herder and Herder, 1968) 7.

5. Rahner, 38.

6. John Paul II, *Mother of the Redeemer*, 14.

7. Joseph Cardinal Ratzinger, "The Sign of the Woman," in *Mary: God's Yes to Man* (San Francisco: Ignatius Press, 1988) 25.

8. Hans Urs von Balthasar, *Mary for Today* (San Francisco: Ignatius Press, 1988) 45.

9. John Paul II, "Aquinas: Defender of Dignity" (7/29/90), *The Pope Speaks* 36:2 (March–April 1991) 80.

Coronation of Mary

Christ in You, the Hope of Glory
Colossians 1:27

The year draws to its dying, leaving behind the fruits of summer's long toil. The harvest is plentiful, but the green of life is gone. Light retreats, and shadows lengthen early. The air grows sharp and cold. The land rests sere and brown; the still waters of lakes and ponds darken under a pale sun barely filtering through dense layers of autumn mists.

The dull, grey light seems to signal the dying of creation: beauty fades; the earth declines to drab existence and decay. In the end all things die. Spring is simply the beginning of the end. Birth, the very gift of life in this world, sets human beings on a journey leading inexorably toward an obscure future moment when some biological reality takes over and life ceases. In the hour of death one must leave everything behind and cross a threshold into a realm far more mysterious than early morning mists shrouding the earth in autumn.

But creation, even as it hurls away toward darkness, holds within itself the seeds of a new harvest to come. And human beings encountering the grey shadows of their own decline toward death still bear the image and likeness of the God who made them. They hold within an eternal seed, one that does not decay into nothingness. Humankind, once ruined by its own doing, is restored to life and wholeness by a loving, merciful Savior. "For God has called man and still calls him so that with his entire being he might be joined to Him in an endless sharing of a divine life beyond all corruption."[1]

As the morning sun lifts the grey mists from the earth, Christ our Savior by his death and resurrection has raised a fallen humanity from the obscurity and nothingness of death. Our Lord stands astride the passageway of death. He is the light that is the life of humankind. He is the eternal seed growing within the human heart to bear lasting fruit.

There are fresh, crisp days in autumn when the great disc of the sun shines clear and brilliant beauty across the blue arches of sky. The deep blue loveliness of the heavens is reflected almost perfectly in the waters of the earth, one endless radiance of light, shining on and on beyond the horizon and the limits of human sight.

On such a day creation sings not a lament for a dying season but praise for the glory of its Creator, for life, and the promise of life forever. On a clear day one seems to see Christ, lighting the world. And one remembers how radiantly that light shone in Mary his mother who was full of grace.

In "The Pool of God"[2] Jessica Powers offers a wonderful image of the one who was blessed above all the women of earth.

> There was nothing in the Virgin's soul
> that belonged to the Virgin—
> no word, no thought, no image, no intent.
> She was a pure, transparent pool reflecting
> God, only God.
> She held His burnished day; she held His night
> of planet-glow or shade inscrutable.

God was her sky and she who mirrored Him
became His firmament.*

Mary of Nazareth, Queen of heaven, like the deep, blue, pure, crystal water shining in the clear light of the morning sun, reflects perfectly the holy radiance of divine life and the fullness of God's presence. In Mary the Holy Spirit found a dwelling place. "For in Mary's faith, first at the Annunciation and then fully at the foot of the Cross, an interior space was reopened within humanity which the eternal Father can fill with every spiritual blessing."³

When Mary left this world, no part of her was empty; no part was dead in sin. Everything Mary did throughout her earthly journey manifested the grace of God. She was the handmaid of the Lord, who mirrored his light for all to see.

In every Christian life there are two moments when we meet our God, *now* and *the hour of our death*. In each succeeding *now* God offers his grace for our salvation, and in the freedom he has given us we may listen to his voice or harden our hearts. All of these moments, the sum of our earthly pilgrimage, are sealed forever in *the hour of our death*. Each now, each today, is preparation for that hour. In Yves Congar's vivid metaphor, life is a precious treasure poured drop by drop like the ointment of Mary Magdalene for our burial. The quality of our death will "depend upon the generosity of the moments that drop by drop have fallen throughout a life lived for God. . . ."⁴

From the now of her beginning to the hour of her death, the Mother of Jesus handed over the treasure of her life to be poured out drop by precious drop in the service of God. She became the Lord's Temple, a space of holiness. Her pas-

---

*Reprinted from *Selected Poetry of Jessica Powers*, copyright © 1989 by Carmelite Monastery of Pewaukee, Wisconsin, edited by Robert F. Morneau and Regina Siegfried, with permission of the publisher, Sheed & Ward, Kansas City, Mo. To order call 1-800-333-7373.

sage from time into eternity simply revealed the glory of God within her, much as the October sun reveals the clear blue brilliance of earth and sky when the hot light of its rays burns away the grey mists of dawn.

This is the meaning we ponder in the last mystery of the rosary, the Coronation of the Mother of God in heaven. Just as the golden halo of light so often found in Christian art signifies sanctity, Mary's crown symbolizes the eternal splendor of divine life radiating from the heart of her being. The Queen of heaven is "our life, our sweetness and our hope," for she is the sign of Christ's triumph over the dark powers pulling creation down to its dying. In Mary the eternal seed has borne fruit that will last. She embodies the reign of God, the coming of his kingdom, and "the riches of the glory of this mystery, which is Christ in you, the hope of glory" (Col 1:27).

Every human being, whether he or she knows it or not, has the hope of glory: "God our Savior desires everyone to be saved and to come to the knowledge of the truth" (1 Tim 2:3-4). The riches of grace and the loving kindness of our God are poured out upon us through his Son our Savior "so that having been justified by his grace, we might become heirs according to the hope of eternal life" (Titus 3:7).

For Christians, who bear within the mystery of Christ and the hope of glory, death is a consequence of life. For us, "living is Christ and dying is gain" (Phil 1:21). To spend the precious ointment of life, to be dispossessed and lose everything because of "the surpassing value of knowing Christ Jesus my Lord," is "to gain Christ and be found in him" (3:7-9). The goal of our life, the end toward which every now is tending, is God. Life once given does not simply terminate or cease; it is a progression, a journey, whose whole meaning is made known in the hour of our death.

When we step from time into eternity, from the now of our seeing as in a darkened mirror into the clear and everlasting light of his glory, we will see him face-to-face. We will know, Paul writes, as we are known. (See 1 Cor 13:12.) "We are God's children now; what we will be has not yet been revealed. What we do know is this: when he is revealed, we will be like him, for we will see him as he is" (1 John 3:2).

In reality the believer already has died. Baptized into Christ's death, we died with him and were buried with him, "so that, just as Christ was raised from the dead by the glory of the Father, so we too might walk in newness of life" (Rom 6:4). In Christ death has no more dominion. In Christ we have overcome death, and are born anew through water and the Holy Spirit. "To overcome death," Romano Guardini wrote, "is to discover in it a meaning which inserts it into the significant whole of life."[5]

Each today of our life, as persons and as the community of Christ, as Church, traces a process of becoming, of growth and maturation toward our end in God, toward that eternal now when God will be everything to everyone (1 Cor 15:28). In our end is our beginning, and life becomes meaningful when we are willing to die and so begin to live. Jesus said, "Those who find their life will lose it, and those who lose their life for my sake will find it" (Matt 10:39). In the process we may "all come to the unity of the faith and of the knowledge of the Son of God, to maturity, to the measure of the full stature of Christ" (Eph 4:13).

The Mother of God is "the image and first flowering of the Church as it is to be perfected in the world to come."[6] The space Mary opened by her faith continues in the Church, in the whole people of God. This is the space of the new and eternal covenant, for the Church is the sign of our union with God and of the unity of all humankind.

Through faith and baptism all of us have put on Christ. We were washed, we were sanctified, we were justified in the name of the Lord Jesus Christ and in the Spirit of our God. (See 1 Cor 6:11.) Having entered into the realm of God's love, we become his holy ones, his saints, for, "In him we live and move and have our being" (Acts 17:28).

Our own human history demonstrates that the real progress of peoples takes place only from the heart, where love and concern for one another is manifested for the good of all. Love is life poured out unceasingly for the other. A heart open to receive and share life-giving love allows holiness, the sanctifying seed of the Spirit given in baptism, to take root and grow, not only in each person but in the community founded in the transcending love of God.

Holiness in essence means that we have been admitted into the realm of divine love, where God offers his grace to us and we receive and share it. Within that center of holiness our Lord's commandment, "Love one another as I have loved you," orders everything. God's love is the standard by which everything is measured. His love inspires and inflames our love. Because divine love embraces all of humankind, our responding love urges us to embrace Christ's mission: I have come that they may have life to the full. Love of God means love of neighbor, and that love gathers everyone within the holy space opened by Mary's faith, within the communion of saints.

Our Lord told his disciples, "I am the way and the truth and the life" (John 14:6). His community is united by their acceptance of his rule, the way of the kingdom. His saints share in his truth; they are sanctified in the truth of the Father's word. (See John 17:17.) And as branches on the vine they draw from the one source the clear spring water of eternal life.

The saints of God may gather around the table of the Lord here on earth, or they may be that fellowship of saints who share the heavenly banquet and sing God's praise with the choirs of heaven. The saints, Father von Balthasar wrote, may already be sanctified so that they cannot sin, or they may be "poor sanctified saints like ourselves, still subject to temptation and sinfulness."[7] In Christ we are made holy by the power of the Spirit, and in a solemn blessing for the Easter season the Church prays for us:

By faith you rose with him in baptism.
May your lives be holy,
so that you will be united with him forever.

The Church is embraced in both the heavenly and the earthly realms. The Queen of Heaven who reveals the Church triumphant in its finest flowering and perfection is one of us, Our Lady St. Mary, in the communion of saints. As the blue waters of a clear lake reflect only the sky directly above, so Mary, the Church, and God's people strive to mirror not the whole Christ who is infinite love, but the fullness of divine life each has received. In the closing lines of "The Pool of God" the poet ponders her own longing to reflect the goodness of God:

> When I so much as turn my thoughts toward her
> my spirit is enisled in her repose.
> And when I gaze into her selfless depths
> an anguish in me grows
> to hold such blueness and to hold such fire.
> I pray to hollow out my earth and be
> filled with these waters of transparency.
> I think that one could die of this desire,
> seeing oneself dry earth or stubborn sod.
> Oh, to become a pure pool like the Virgin,
> water that lost the semblances of water
> and was a sky like God.[8]

The Virgin Mary reminds us that, ". . . it is by the light of the saints, which is nothing other than God's light in the world, that we see *the* Light."[9]

The presence of the Light, the fact of our salvation and sanctification in Christ, presents every human being, every Christian, with a choice and a standard. We are free to respond to God or to reject him. The invited guests, for example, refused to attend the wedding banquet the king gave for his son's marriage. Others were invited on the day of the feast so that the wedding hall would be filled. But these guests, pulled from the streets, had to prepare themselves for the banquet by donning a wedding garment. (See Matt 22:2-14.)

The saints also prepare to enter the banquet hall of the king by manifesting their love for God and one another, for love, the seamless garment of charity, is the norm of holiness. The world must glimpse in the Church and its members the love with which Christ suffered to redeem it. Thus Christ, the love of God himself, is the standard against which our life is measured. He is the one appointed by the Father to return on the clouds of heaven at the end of time to judge the living and the dead.

We judge ourselves in one sense. When we pass from this world to the next we will see him as he is and know as we have been known. In other words, our meeting with the Lord will show us how clearly we have reflected him, how faithfully we have lived the grace that has been our portion along the way to the kingdom of heaven.

Jesus, when he commanded his disciples to love one another as he had loved them, added these words: "No one has greater love than this, to lay down one's life for one's friends" (John 15:13). The sign of the world's salvation is the cross on which Jesus poured out his own life to redeem us, bearing the guilt of each one he judges. In the moment of his death God's Son opened the enclosed space of the old covenant and the boundaries imposed by sin and death. Mark records that when Jesus breathed his last, "The curtain of the temple was torn in two, from top to bottom" (15:38). The tearing of the curtain, which covered the entrance to the Holy of Holies, opened a holy space where heaven and earth meet, a space open to the world Jesus came to save. To the Crucified Savior no one stands outside the embrace of the Cross, and thus no one stands outside the holy space where love is life poured out unceasingly for others.

In the world, however, the Cross stands precisely where people exist outside that circle of life. It is there, among the sinners, the hopeless, and the dying, that Christ's love founds his community within the space opened by the faith of his mother and the disciple whom he loved. There a center is created from which the mystery of Christ in us, our hope of glory, may become reality for everyone.

Our Lord challenges all who are baptized in his name to enter the holy space where heaven and earth meet, to lay down their own lives in order to bear his life-giving love to all the world whatever the cost: "Are you able to drink the cup that I drink, or be baptized with the baptism that I am baptized with?" (Mark 10:38).

The Cross calls the believer to leave the walled security of the Holy City and go to Christ outside the gate, where people are abandoned, despised, divided, ignorant of God, or atheistic. The communion of saints moves continually outward, for Christ's Church is an open society whose members fill the "absence" of God with his presence and bear hope into situations of hopelessness. The voices of the saints go out to all the earth, and their words proclaim salvation to the ends of the world.

In the light of the Cross the love uniting God's people in the communion of saints becomes visible, tangible. Beneath the Cross we pass from death to life, because we believe in the Son of God and love one another. That is why the saints are found most often in situations where hopelessness, poverty, atheism, and death abound. They tend the sick, pull the dying from the streets, feed the hungry, find shelter for the homeless, visit the imprisoned, comfort the anguished and embittered wanderers of our earth. We find them in situations of life as well, nurturing and providing for a family, teaching children, counseling young and old. When we recall that Paul referred to all Christians as "saints," we recognize the seriousness of our own commitment through our baptism to holiness and sanctity.

Relying on the abundant gifts of the Spirit, the saints have willingly dispossessed themselves to be consumed by God and the mission he gives them. They leave the sacred center, go outside, to bear if they must the abuse our Lord endured, in order to share the precious treasure of life to the last fragrant drop.

The Letter of James addresses the reader bluntly:

> What good is it, my brothers and sisters, if you say you have faith but do not have works? Can faith save you? So faith by itself, if it has no works, is dead. But someone will say, "You have faith and I have works." Show me your faith apart from your works, and I by my works will show you my faith.
>
> 2:14, 17, 18

Jesus taught his disciples, "Not everyone who says to me, 'Lord, Lord,' shall enter the kingdom of heaven." One may prophesy, cast out demons, and do many mighty works in Jesus' name; but if the service is superficial and without love, it is nothing. The Lord and Judge will declare to them, "I never knew you; go away from me, you evildoers" (Matt 7:21-23).

In the dramatic judgment scene (Chapter 25) of Matthew's Gospel the Son of man, the Christ enthroned in glory, does not ask the people gathered before him: What wonders did you work? or, How much did you suffer for me? He asks instead: Did you see me when I was hungry and thirsty, when I was a stranger in your land, when I was naked, sick, or imprisoned, when I had nothing to sustain life? Did you see that I was suffering in your brother, that I was your lost and lonely sister, that I was denied human dignity and left for dead? And did you then offer me the help I needed to live, did you raise me up, did you share the love that gives you life and so restore me to the land of the living?

Our holiness is measured by our response to the call to share the richness that is the gift of life with others, our willingness to bring the light of Christ where he is not, to recognize him where he does not seem to be, to find him where we were not seeking him. That is what Mary of

Nazareth did when she bore Christ into the world. She was the one to whom God entrusted the mystery of salvation, as he entrusts it to his Church and his people today.

The grace that is ours in baptism guides and sustains our life journey and just as surely leads us home. Because we are sanctified by the grace of God, we live within that sphere of triune love, the communion of Father, Son, and Holy Spirit. St. Thomas Aquinas said that glory is grace at home. Thus ". . . we should not be surprised if, when we 'enter heaven' after death, we find we have already been there without noticing it."[10]

It is in company with the least of his brothers and sisters that our Lord will seek his people when "the Son of man comes in his glory and all the angels with him." And when he sees them, he will place them on his right and say, "Come, you that are blessed by my Father, inherit the kingdom prepared for you from the foundation of the world" (Matt 25:31, 34).

In the hour of our death, when the last drop is poured out for our burial, God will lift his own into the new creation that does not pass away and enfold us together with Mary our Mother and the whole communion of saints in the eternal love of the Father, Son, and Spirit. The kingdom will come. And the mystery of Christ in us, our hope of glory, will be revealed as light breaking forth and shining like the sun in our heavenly Father's realm through an unending, perfect day.

NOTES

1. *Pastoral Constitution on the Church in the Modern World*, 18.
2. Jessica Powers, "The Pool of God," in *Selected Poetry of Jessica Powers*, Regina Siegfried and Robert Morneau, eds. (Kansas City, Mo.: Sheed & Ward, 1989) 63.
3. John Paul II, *Mother of the Redeemer*, 28.
4. Yves Conger, O.P., *Faith and the Spiritual Life*, 213.

5. Romano Guardini, *Death of Socrates*, trans. Basil Wrighton (Cleveland: The World Publishing Company, 1962) 89.

6. *Dogmatic Constitution on the Church*, 68.

7. Hans Urs von Balthasar, *You Crown the Year with Your Goodness: Sermons through the Liturgical Year*, trans. Graham Harris (San Francisco: Ignatius Press, 1989) 200.

8. Powers, *Selected Poetry*, 63.

9. Balthasar, *You Crown the Year*, 212.

10. Ibid., 200.

Epilogue: Mary Mother of the Church

> Mother and Child
> Earth and Heaven in little space,
> Their love-fire glows from winter's hearth
> And lights our way home.

The image of Mother and Child symbolizes more profoundly than any other sign of human existence our hope and yearning for life in a world dominated by the reality of death. The vast, rich treasure house of Christian art includes iconographic masterpieces of the Virgin Mary with her Child Jesus. Carved, painted, inlaid, cut, woven, embroidered, printed, fired, baked, sketched, or photographed, these icons express the wonder of the incarnation while drawing the believer deeper into the mystery of our redemption in Christ. They reflect the reverent, often poignant love of Christians for the Lord Jesus and his mother, and their trust in the promise of his kingdom.

The image of Mother and Child holds natural meaning as well as artistic beauty and inspiration. Mother and Child are a sign of unity; together they suggest a comforting wholeness, the oneness of heart that cherishes and fosters life itself. In a world where death seems to be the rule, Mother and Child reveal that life endures by affirming its continuity from one generation to another. They are a natural sign of life and hope.

Existence depends upon relationship, on the intricate interweaving of countless interdependencies among the physical entities making up the universe of creation. Human life is impossible outside the relationship of two beings, the man and the woman. In Genesis both are necessary in the creation of humankind; both are formed in the image and likeness of God. Together they form the wholeness, the integrity of humankind. As father and mother they assure humanity's continuing existence in another generation; they constitute its genetic and cultural heritage.

The process of continuity, the actual birth and development of new life, is a material one. It is from the mother that a child draws the materials essential for its development and growth toward maturity. In motherhood we see a visible expression of creation's continuity. The Latin word for mother, *mater*, comes "by a divine pun like *Eva* and *Ave*,"[1] from *materia* meaning *matter*, the stuff of creation, the material world that forms the substance of life.

In the Genesis story of creation the woman receives her name, Eve, mother of the living, after the fall and the pronouncing of God's judgment. This, Cardinal Ratzinger suggests, is significant. The woman "preserves the mystery of life, the power opposed to death. . . ." She "who bears the key of life, thus touches directly the mystery of being, the living God."[2] We can understand motherhood as continuity not only with the material world of creation, but also with the Creator on whom that world depends for existence.

When the Son of the Creator-God came to redeem his fallen creation, he entered the world as a human being through the material process of birth.

> But when the fullness of time had come, God sent his Son, born of woman, born under the law, in order to redeem those who were under the law, so that we might receive adoption as children.
>
> Galatians 4:4-5

Paul here expresses the heritage of the world redeemed in the Incarnate Word of God. While these are logical, quiet words, the vastness of their meaning seems almost to explode from their simplicity.

Creation already holds something of eternity. God descended into the material world and took to himself the stuff of creation, becoming a child of flesh and blood within the womb of the Virgin Mary. This seemingly impossible motherhood becomes the sign of the world's salvation. The image of Mary and Jesus symbolizes the unity of redeemed creation within the divine oneness of God the Father, Son, and Holy Spirit. This woman, the Virgin Mother full of grace, with her holy Child touches the mystery of being, the living God.

All this is the work of the Holy Spirit, the Breath on which God's Word is borne into the world, the power by which the Word is active among us. Mary herself expresses the reality of that material world; she is the key witness to the humanity of Jesus. Through her, our faith as Christians is rooted firmly in the earth, in the creation redeemed by her son. At the same time, Mary's motherhood reveals the grace and power of God redeeming the material world of matter. She is the one on whom the power of the Most High descended, and her child is the fruit of the Holy Spirit overshadowing her.

Christians too are the work of the Holy Spirit. "It belongs to the Father to procreate in his likeness (cf. Rom 8:29), but the children made in his image are born to him in the Spirit, and it is in the Spirit that they grow and live as sons."[3] Our communion with God and our adoption as his children are brought about in the Spirit. In baptism we receive the Spirit. Christ, wrote St. Leo the Great, "has given to water what he had given to his Mother; the power of the Most High and the overshadowing of the Holy Spirit, which was responsible for Mary's bringing forth the Saviour, has the same effect, so that water may regenerate the believer."[4]

The Holy Spirit is the love uniting the Father and the Son. That divine love is reflected in the material world reborn in the Spirit and made whole again. This is the grace of God in his Incarnate Word gathering a people to himself, incorporating those reborn in baptism into the one body of his Church.

We receive the Spirit, Paul wrote, by hearing the Word with faith, and by faith we receive the promise of the Spirit. (See Gal 3:2, 14.) The love of God poured into our hearts by the Spirit is the blessing of life. By the fact of their faith believers are open to the creative power of God, to the love that will not let us go, the love that endures beyond the time and space of material existence into the eternity of Father, Son, and Spirit.

> Therefore, since we are justified by faith, we have peace with God through our Lord Jesus Christ, through whom we have obtained access to this grace in which we stand; and we boast in our hope of sharing the glory of God.
>
> Romans 5:1-2

What happens to believers "is first fully brought about in Christ."[5] The Spirit overshadowing Mary establishes her as the Mother of God; the Word is made flesh within her by the creative power of God. The gift of the Spirit to Christians in baptism means that the Word is present and active within the person who believes. The Word is, as it were, enfleshed in the disciple who is open continually to receive the grace of the Spirit.

At his death Jesus gave his disciples the gift of the Spirit and the gift of his own mother who received the disciple her son loved as her own child. Mary thus is Mother of the Church, and she is the image of the Church as the Mother who, overshadowed by the Spirit of Pentecost, brings forth the children of God in history.

"It can be said that from Mary the Church also learns her own motherhood," writes John Paul II. "If the Church is the sign and instrument of intimate union with God, she is so by reason of her motherhood, because receiving life from the Spirit, she 'generates' sons and daughters of the human race to new life in Christ."[6] The woman clothed with the sun, with the moon under her feet, and on her head a crown of twelve stars, who cried out in the agony of giving birth can be understood as the sign of the Church laboring to bring forth the children of God. (See Rev 12:1-2.)

In Christ the children of God live and move and have their being. Those who have heard the Word, who have received the seed of the Word in the fertile soil that fosters its growth toward the harvest, constitute his Church. They live also in and through the Church, and the Church lives in them.

In the life of the Church one sees again the image of Mother and Child as the promise and the hope of eternal life. While Mary, the Mother of God, stands as the great image of the Church as Mother, the Church as the body of Christ endures in history and moves toward the final coming of the kingdom in the children born to her of the Spirit. Because God came to redeem us as we are, because he entered our human existence through the material reality of Mary, the world has become the place where we encounter his living presence throughout our human history.

The Christian, wrote Father von Balthasar:

> is conscious of sharing in the continual transformation from the darkness of this world into the light of the next. What ultimately decides if the salvation proclaimed is the true one is the fact that it does not merely come down from above on a lost world, ripe for judgment, but rather acts upon it. God's grace in fact is bestowed on the world so that, filled with divine power, it may—groaningly and in pain—struggle through into the light of eternity.[7]

Thus God asks of us what he asked of Mary. He also promises that what he does for Mary he will do for each of us. Mary is our mother, the mother who forgets neither her children nor her own humanity. She is material creation completely open to the life-giving presence of God. She proclaims the saving work of God in our fallen-redeemed world.

The Virgin Mary with her holy Child reveals how deeply God has descended for love of us into our history. The Child in Mary's arms is set for the fall and the rising of many. He is King of kings and Lord of lords; he holds the keys of life and death; his power is infinite. Within the tender embrace of those loving arms the Child is also weak and vulnerable, dependent for continuing existence on the material reality of his Mother.

Within this Child is the wisdom of ages, the grace of eternity, the goodness and compassion of the God who is love. To us, as well as his mother, he offers the breath of life to make of us temples of the Spirit, dwelling places of the Most High, children of God who hold fast to the word of life and "shine like stars in the world" (Phil 2:15).

Mary invites us into the heart of the incarnation to be enfolded within the mystery of Being, of Father, Son, and Holy Spirit of love. She whose eyes see the living God invites us to come and see where he stays, where he lives. Mother and Child together, earth and heaven in little space, are light and hope and life for us. For the one who by grace truly sees Jesus believes in him, and, believing, already has entered eternal life.

> Pray for us, O Holy Mother of God
> that we may be made worthy
> of the promises of Christ.

NOTES

1. Mary E. and Leon J. Podles, "The Feminine and Universal Salvation," *America* 163:2 (10/27/90) 296.
2. Joseph Cardinal Ratzinger, *Daughter Zion*, trans. John McDermott, S.J. (San Francisco: Ignatius Press, 1983) 17.
3. Durrwell, *Holy Spirit of God*, 152.
4. In Paul VI, *Devotion to the Blessed Virgin Mary*, 19.
5. Durrwell, 153.
6. *Mother of the Redeemer*, 43.
7. Hans Urs von Balthasar, *Exploration in Theology I: The Word Made Flesh*, trans. A. V. Littledale with Alexander Dru (San Francisco: Ignatius Press, 1989) 109.

Concluding Prayers

Queen of the Most Holy Rosary,
pray for us.

May the Virgin Mary with her Holy Child
bless us.

May the blessing of almighty God,
Father, Son, and Holy Spirit,
descend upon us
and remain with us forever.

Amen.

Guide to Flower Illustrations

Crocuses   (Prologue, p. 3)
Forsythia   (p. 10)

Lily of the Valley   (Annunciation, p. 11)
Forget-Me-Not   (Visitation, p. 22)
Shooting Star   (Birth of Jesus, p. 33)
Daffodil   (Presentation of the Lord, p. 44)
Cornflower   (Finding Jesus in the Temple, p. 55)

Hawthorne branch   (Interlude, p. 66)
Bleeding Heart   (Jesus' Agony, p. 77)
Bloodroot   (Jesus Is Scourged, p. 88)
Wild Rose   (Jesus Is Crowned, p. 100)
Campanula   (Jesus Carries the Cross, p. 112)
Scarlet Anemone   (Jesus Dies on the Cross, p. 124)

Peach Tree Branch   (Interlude, p. 135)
Madonna Lily   (Resurrection, p. 145)
Columbine   (Ascension, p. 157)
Blaze of Fire Salvia   (Coming of the Spirit, p. 170)
Moss Rose   (Assumption of Mary, p. 182)
Gloriosa Daisy   (Coronation, p. 193)

Japanese Anemones   (Epilogue, p. 205)